Put fence to Stress

(551 possible remedies without Pharmacopoeia)

Compiled and written by:

José Enrique Centén Martín

Legal deposit: M-007429/2018

Cover image: ©JECM

The genesis

There is no better cure than that offered by nature, but ignorance and above all for comfort, we uset to the pharmacopoeia when we have available food that can remedy our ills and is what I capture in this book. It is very common to abuse or misinterpret the phrase of Horacio (65 - 8 B.C.) when he said **"Carpe Diem,** quam minimim credula postero", they do it or we did it when we were young, normal time of rebellion, but the passage from adolescence to full maturity, which is not so great, without correcting that adolescent error is when you can enter imbalances generated by today's society, where competitiveness, success, lack of stable work, or not according to your needs, by precarious, can cause health problems by abusing prescribed or advised Pharmacopoeia, and it can lead to even greater problems, addictions, anxiety, depression or other more pernicious imbalances. Even for groups of: **Security, Rescue, Hospital, or Teaching,** given the pressure they endure in their careers.

Following the advice of Hipócrates de Cós (460 - 370 B.C.), **"Let food be your food and your food your medicine",** basic advice to comply with, for sure we have all taken infusions or foods recommended by relatives and ancestors, being effective for some specific ailment, for that reason I ventured to write a book (in Spanish - 8256 Remedios Naturales) titled 8256 Natural Remedies, for the 170 most common ailments that we suffer, and from him I have made the present monograph, are not only herbal remedies, there are fruits, vegetables, legumes, roots, trees known in their vast majority, all with great benefits for our health to be used as food or tisanes in many cases, with the purpose that this book is a remedy for the problems we suffer, since for each ailment there are several proposals and hardly any will not go well.

Let us follow the teachings of the ancients, as defined by the Spanish proverb: **"From the hive the honey and from the mouth of the wise, the knowledge".**

Presentation

Stress is one of the typical disorders of today's society, saturated with work, responsibilities and information, and for 6% of the population it becomes a problem. **At the year about 60 million of Benzodiazepines are consumed, being** on many occasions cause of addictions, serious hepatic and nervous disorders. Remedies are offered here with medicinal plants being a healthy **method to alleviate these serious problems and the vast majority without contraindications. Palliative remedies with 258 plants for: Stress (68) and other associated symptoms such as: Anxiety (57), Depressions (57), Headaches (68), Insomnia (75), Sick headache (10), Migraines (30), Sedatives (132).** In this book **is also included an ailment of unknown origin Fibromyalgia (12)** that can **derive in some tables described above.** Added something unusual but important, **Detoxifying (32),** that in some cases of stress may have caused **addictions to Tobacco, Drugs, Alcohol, Ludopathies or Medication. Also a final section entitled Sweeteners, for our drinks with something other than sugar (without nutritional contribution to health).**

Index of Ailments

Stress

- **Ashwagandha,** combat stress and the central nervous system, **caution those who take medications for the same effect,** especially barbiturates, also acts against anxiety, see **description of the plant,** form of use **VII.**

- **Ayahuasca,** the cooking of its leaves, stem and seeds, in infusion, is the method for stress and adjacent remedies, see **description of the plant,** form of use **VII.**

- **Baikal skullcap,** the infusion of 3 or 4 sprigs of fresh, three times a day, combats stress and daily tensions, as well as anxiety, see **description plant.**

- **Banana,** for its vitamin B content, it is very good to calm the nervous system, especially in times of **stress or anguish,** eat bananas as a snack in these cases. Consider that their consumption, the content Tryptophan becomes Serotonin, is beneficial against **depression,** see **description plant.**

- **Barley,** use in decoction to drink in situations of stress, to produce a greater consumption and excretion of minerals (Potassium, Calcium, Magnesium) and vitamins, especially group B, see **description of the plant,** form of use **VII**

- **Beet,** cooked helps to overcome stress, see **description of the plant.**

- **Blue passionflower,** it is adequate to avoid the involuntary pain and spasms produced **by stress, in cases of anxiety** it is a light anxiolytic, **and without dependence risk,** its effect being also important to **calm seasonal depression,** and adequate **for headaches,** even in neuralgia, see **description of the plant,** form of use **VII.**

- **Briar root,** as a **sedative** it helps to calm nervous states in case of **stress and anxiety.** For the health of persons with **depression and fatigue,** see **description of the plant.**

- **Calamintha,** 1 single drop of its essence orally relieves stress, see **description of the plant.**

- **Cassava, Yuca or Manioc,** the components extracted from the crust help in the protection against oxidative stress, see **description of the plant.**

- **Cedar oil,** when needed, inspire two times directly from the package to reduce stress, see **description of the plant.**

- **Chickpea,** adequate consumption in situations of stress and irritability, see **description of the plant.**

- **Clary or Clary sage,** inhaled oil is the ideal resource in times of challenge or personal changes, especially when there is external **stress or extreme pressure.** During the **crisis of mature age** its oil exerts a balancing, encouraging and revitalizing influence. In situations full of stress, this oil reduces the tension of internal origin, decreases the speed of the accelerated mind and calms the nerves. By restoring inner tranquility, it **minimizes the debilitating effects of stress** and the related ailments. Reduces **irritability, panic attacks,** by reviving worn nerves. It also reduces muscle pain resulting from mental or emotional stress and nervous tension, see **description of the plant,** form of use **VII (2).**

- **Common poppy,** regular and daily consumption of their seeds are especially recommended in situations of **stress, insomnia problems,** acting as a natural sedative, see **description of the plant,** form of consume **VIII.**

- **Escarole or Tarragon,** it has a high content of vitamin C and is rich in potassium, helps to prevent stress, see **description of the plant.**

- **Estragon,** so much for **stress situations as for headaches,** take a teaspoon of dried Estragon dry per cup of infused water (can be taken without limits), or add it fresh and finely chopped to meals, see **description of the plant.**

- **Fragrant incense or Plectranthus,** if used with sandalwood (herb), it reassures cases of stress or nervousness, **only burnt,** see **description of the plant.**

- **Geranium or Cranesbills,** Ingested is very appreciated to relieve stress, see **description of the plant,** form of use **VII.**

- **Ginger,** consume, because having a substance called Cineol helps to reduce anxiety, the first symptoms of stress take an infusion, see **description of the plant.**

- **Green tea,** the soothing effect combined with the scent of Jasmine is very beneficial to **relieve stress and anxiety,** see **description of the different plants.**

- **Hazel,** against stress, infusions reduce symptoms, see **description of the plant,** form of use **VII.**

- **Hazelnut,** your group B vitamins alleviate different symptoms of **stress, anxiety and depression,** see **description of the plant.**

- **Hop,** se le otorga beneficios notables para quien padece **estrés y síntomas de ansiedad**, see **description of the plant,** form of use **VII.**

- **Jamaica pepper,** its consumption is used to **relieve stress,** in **cases of depression** alleviates emotional sadness, by its pleasant smell that floods the senses and makes you feel better, see **description of the plant.**

- **Jasmine,** see in **Green tea,** see **description of the plant.**

- **Kiwi,** helps to lower stress, by intervening in the water balance inside and outside the nerve cell, see **description of the plant.**

- **Korean ginseng or Chinese ginseng,** it is important for those who suffer from **stress and anxiety,** see **description of the plant.**

- **Kudzu,** of relaxing properties, **combats excessive stress,** and helps create a relaxed mood in emotions, see **description of the plant.**

- **Lamb´s lettuce,** belongs to the family of Valerian, being beneficial to control anxiety is used to balance the nervous system, very convenient in case of **stress and anxiety,** see **description of the plant.**

- **Lavender,** as a frequent tonic it can help **in conditions of fatigue, and stress**. Lavender flower Water cloths reduce pain levels, the smell of Lavender can **reduce headaches,** see **description of the plant.**

- **Lice-Bane or Stavesacre,** indispensable because of the **addiction to sex or onamism.** It can heal, **hypochondria and hysteria** that have their starting point in the sexual organs due to libidinous excesses whose consequences are profoundly debilitating, and against the neuroses caused by enervating moral emotions by excitations that start from within, like the poorly supported indignation and grief that **causes stress. It is also used against** headaches or continuous stun, **caution,** see **description plant.**

- **Maca,** it is a support to the adrenal glands, maintaining the general health of the body in situations of stress. Regulates and increases the function of the endocrine system, in the glands that produce the hormones necessary for bodily functions, even in the mood of **depression, for the headache** is of analgesic effect thanks to the Terpenoids and Saponins, see **description of the plant.**

- **Mayten,** to treat the symptoms of stress, put 10 gr. in ½ liter of water, boil 10 minutes, filter and drink hot, see **description of the plant.**

- **Naranjilla,** reduces stress and anxiety by causing hormonal changes that trigger state of mind and a pleasant disposition. It affects the levels of corticosterone hormone stress, see **description of the plant.**

- **Narrow-leaf strap fern,** for nervous disorders, insomnia and stress in infusions or as daytime water, see **description of the plant,** form of use **VII.**

- **Nectarine,** a component of the Nectarine is Magnesium, a mineral that balances the central nervous system and it provides a sedative action, so it is recommended in moments of stress, see **description of the plant.**

- **Neroli oil,** inhaling a few drops in diffuser, combat **stress and depression,** relieve tension and raise good mood, see **description of plant.**

- **Pomegranate,** consume to relieve stress, see **description of the plant, form of consume VIII.**

- **Rose,** it is used in infusion to **reduce stress** and relieve feelings of resentment, and **in depression** it calms the symptoms and alleviates feelings of regret, jealousy, see **description of the plant.**

- **Saffron crocus,** drink a cup of infusion with 0.5 gr. in 250 ml. of boiling water, for **stress and anxiety,** see **description of the plant.**

- **Sumatra benzoin tree,** against **stress and anxiety** can be used internally or, in inhalations its essential oil, see **description of the plant.**

- **Soursop,** the chewed leaves have a high sedative power, effectively serving to **calm the nerves, stress, headaches** and in case of mild insomnia to sleep better, see **description of the plant.**

- **Southern magnolia or Bull bay,** it has certain anxiolytic qualities that directly impact the hormonal balance of the body, **especially in stress,** able to **reduce anxiety and stress** by calming the mind. It also relieves depression, by stimulating the release of Dopamine and the hormones of "pleasure", turning the state of mind in a short time, see **description plant.**

- **Sweetscented bedstraw,** this species is a good sedative and hypnotic of proven effects as a soothing, it can be used in **situations of stress, and depression,** see **description of the plant,** form of use **VII.**

- **Turmeric,** consumed in powder stimulates the nervous system, has effects on the immune system and mood by causing an increase in the production of Serotonin, see **description of the plant.**

- **Vervain,** use **for stress,** acts against **depression, melancholy** and apathy, see **description of the plant,** form of use **VII (2).**

- **Vitex or Chaste tree,** the infusion reduces the level of estrogen in the adrenal glands that cause stress, see **description of the plant.**

- **Water lilies or Nymphaea,** its oil in topical use is used as **anti-stress,** against nervous tension and **depression,** see **description of the plant.**

- **West Indian cherry,** its consumption produces hormones such as Melatonin, and maintenance of the gland that secretes Adrenaline, especially during periods of **high stress, against anxiety and depression.** Its anti-inflammatory properties by Anthocyanins help to cure **migraines and headaches,** in the same way that an Aspirin or an Ibuprofen helps us. To regulate **sleep cycles or insomnia,** it helps to produce hormones such as Melatonin, see **description of the plant.**

- **Withania aristata,** the infusion of the root crust is used to combat stress, **caution,** see **description of the plant.**

- **Wood violet,** it is used against nervous stress, see **description of the plant,** form of use **VII.**

- **Yarrow,** one of the most recommended plants in cases of depression taking infusions 2 or 3 times a day. Good system also in **cases of anxiety, stress or nerves,** see **description of the plant,** form of use **VII.**

- **Ylang Ylang,** perform massage for relaxation in situations **of stress and as an antidepressant** is a deep relaxant, **caution,** see **description of plant.**

- **Finally,** we describe the plants that only **the simple infusion is necessary to ingest, to combat cases of Stress the:**
Bitter orange, Evergreen oak, Lemon verbena, Marsh skullcap, Orange, Perilla or Deulkkae, Red clover Rooibos, Salep drink, Siberian ginseng, Silver wattle or Mimosa, Small-leaved lime, Vetiver, Virginia water horehound and European bugleweed or Gypsywort.
The **plants can be potentiated** with others for same ailment, but it is **always convenient to remember,** the perfect use of each plant according **to its description,** in case there is any **interaction with drugs or posible contraindications.**

Anxiety

The plants, **Ashwagandha or Indian ginseng, Baikal skullcap, Ginseng, Green tea, Hazelnut, Hop, Jasmine, Kava, Lamb´s lettuce, Naranjilla, Rose or Gallic rose, Saffron crocus, Small-leaved lime, Southern magnolia or Bull bay, Sumatra benzoin tree, West Indian cherry,** plants used as anxiety are included **in the Stress section.**

- **Artichoke,** is good against anxiety, see **description of the plant,** form of consume in **VIII.**

- **Bergamot orange,** when consuming the fruit or taking in infusion it helps in case of anxiety, see **description of the plant.**

- **Bitter orange,** in infusion is an excellent natural anxiolytic that Nature can give us, acts on the organs that are affected by cases of anxiety and mood swing, see **description of the plant.**

- **Blue passionflower,** in cases of anxiety it is a light anxiolytic, and without risk of dependence, see **description of the plant,** form of use **VII.**

- **Brazil nut,** for cases of anxiety, distress, see **description of the plant.**

- **Butterbur,** infusion for disorders of anxiety, anguish, caution, see **description of the plant.**

- **Clary or Clary sage,** Its oil mitigates the anxiety and emotional tension that often accompanies asthma attacks, see **description of the plant.**

- **Fragrant incense or Plectranthus,** used with lemon improves anxiety states, single burnt, see **description of the plant.**

- **Garlic,** 4 garlic a day help reduce anxiety and nerves, see **description of the plant.**

- **Ginger,** consume in any way, because having a substance called Cineole helps to reduce anxiety, see **description of the plant.**

- **Grape vine,** the leaves in infusion, made with the decoction of a teaspoon of dried leaves per cup of water for 10 minutes, rest for 10 minutes and take every quarter of an hour 1 tablespoon, see **description of the plant.**

- **Indian sandalwood,** to calm anxiety, see **description of the plant.**

- **Japanese buckwheat,** its richness in carbohydrates, vitamins of group B, magnesium and lysine, is recommended in case of anxiety, see **description of the plant,** form of consume **VIII.**

- **Jasmine,** see **en Gree tea,** see **description of the plant.**

- **Lemon balm or Melissa,** being slightly hypnotic and **sedative**, it fights the specific anxiety attacks, see **description of the plant.**

- **Lemon,** combat anxiety, see **description of the plant.**

- **Motherwort,** in infusion has properties against anxiety, or unrest, see **description of the plant,** form of use **VII.**

- **Neroli oil,** inhaled or in diffusion, has relaxing and soothing effect on the mind and body as anxiety, see **description of the plant.**

- **Peanut,** a handful of peanuts generates pleasant levels of Serotonin that the brain interprets as a feeling of well-being for cases of anxiety, see **description of the plant.**

- **Perforate St John's-wort,** the infusion acts against anxiety as a sedative. Also the encapsulated powder, see **description of the plant,** form of use **VII (1).**

- **Red pepper,** contain vitamin B6 and Magnesium, this combination reduces anxiety, see **description of the plant.**

- **Silver wattle or Mimosa,** relaxes in case of anxiety and nervous tension, see **description of the plant.**

- **Vervain,** use to combat anxiety, see **description of the plant,** form of use **VII (2).**

- **Virginia water horehound,** for those persons who suffer from unexplained anxiety can be very effective, see **description of the plant.**

- **Finally,** we describe the plants that only **the simple infusion to ingest or consumption,** for anxiety problems:
Briar root, Chamomile or Camomile, Sweet flag or Calamus, Garden angelica, Honeysuckles, Indian pennywort, Large-leaved lime, Lemon verbena, Marjoram, Marsh skullcap, Peony or Paeony, Perilla or Deulkkae, Spearmint, Sumbal or Muskroot, Yellow trumpetbush, Vanilla, Vitex or Chaste tree.

It can **also be potentiated** with different plants for the same ailment, but it is convenient **to always remember** the perfect use of each plant used according **to its description,** in case there is any **interaction with drugs or possible contraindications.**

Depressions

The plants, **Banana, Blue passionflower, Briar root, Hazelnut, Jamaica pepper or Allspice, Maca, Neroli oil, Rose, Southern magnolia or Bull bay, Sweetscented bedstraw, Vervain, Water lilies or Nymphaea, West Indian cherry, Ylang Ylang,** plants used as depressions are included **in the Stress section.**

Continue on next page

- **Artichoke,** it is good for nervous disorders, such as depression, see **description of the plant,** form of consume **VIII.**

- **Barley,** the decoction to drink in cases of asthenia, spring fatigue or depression, see **description of the plant,** form of use **VII.**

- **Bergamot orange,** the fruit, the infusion and the diluted oil are antidepressants, due to their psychotropic characteristics, see **description of the plant.**

- **Bitter kola,** his oil paled the symptoms of depression. Before using **(it is important to consult a medical specialist),** see **description of the plant.**

- **Bitter orange,** the infusion is effective to relieve cases of depression, see **description of the plant.**

- **Borage,** the infusion is used for emotional fatigue, melancholy and depression, see **description of the plant,** form of use **VII.**

- **Brazil nut,** moderate intake is beneficial in depression, see **description of the plant.**

- **Cacao or Cocoa,** the presence of Phenylethylamine, the production of Endorphins, for a state of emotional well-being and euphoria, see **description of the plant.**

- **Chamomile or Camomile,** useful to alleviate the physical effects of depression, see **description of the plant.**

- **Cherimoya,** of tonic action that prevents decay and fatigue, avoiding depressions, see **description of the plant.**

- **Chestnut fruit,** its amount of Phosphorus gets better mood during the day. **Help fight apathy and melancholy,** see **description of the plant.**

- **Chestnut tree,** to combat depression, asthenia or long convalescence, see **description of the plant,** form of use **VII (1).**

- **Chickpea,** adequate legume in situations of asthenia or nervous depression, see **description of the plant.**

- **Chicory,** It is good to treat fatigue and depression problems, see **description of the plant,** form of use **VII.**

- **Chives,** helps to treat fatigue, asthenia and depression, see **description of the plant.**

- **Clary or Clary sage,** its oil inhaled, restores emotional balance, reduces melancholy and depression, see **description of the plant.**

- **Cowslip primrose,** to treat depression, see **description of the plant,** form of use **VII.**

- **Fragrant incense or Plectranthus,** with Orange blossom (flower of the Orange tree or Lemon tree) or Jasmine helps to lift and balance emotions, improving mood, only burnt, see **descriptions of the plants.**

- **Geranium or Cranesbills,** ingested is very appreciated to relieve stress and depression, see **description of the plant,** form of use **VII.**

- **Gingko,** in mild depressive processes of elderly persons, associated with cerebral insufficiency and reduction of Serotonin, neurotransmitter in nerve cells, see **description of the plant.**

- **Ginseng,** It is important for those suffering from depression, see **description of the plant.**

- **Goldenseal,** in the case of a great Depression, **or leads to think of suicide,** it is a very used remedy, precaution, see **description of the plant.**

- **Great morinda or Noni,** consume against **mental depression,** see description of the plant. Depression, see **description of the plant.**

- **Gree tea,** regular consumption can help speed up mood and depression, see **description of the plant.**

- **Herb Bennet,** the roots serve to combat depression and asthenia, see **description of the plant,** form of use **VII (1).**

- **Hogweed,** its action against depression is mainly due to asthenics, see **description of the plant,** form of use **VII.**

- **Indian pennywort,** use against depressive disorders, see **description of the plant.**

- **Indian sandalwood,** it is used to fight depression, see **description of the plant.**

- **Japanese buckwheat,** its richness in carbohydrates, vitamins of group B, Magnesium and Lysine, is recommended in case **of depression or generalized fatigue,** see **description of the plant,** form of consume **VIII.**

- **Kava,** the infusion is convenient to use in case of nervous depression, **caution,** see **description of the plant.**

- **Lemon,** for cases of depression, see **description of the plant.**

- **Lice-Bane or Stavesacre,** persons subjected a long time to the painful emotions of grief with spite and irascibility, weakened, cachectic, it is effective in **sadness and hypochondriacal melancholy,** annihilation of the sensation as of **tiredness and fatigue** on awakening, **caution,** see **description of the plant.**

- **Martagon lily or Turk's cap lily,** the infusion of the bulbs is used for depressive treatments, see **description of the plant.**

- **Orange,** its variety of nutrients help to have a good vital tone and to scare away apathy and discouragement, see **description of the plant.**

- **Peach,** its properties improve the depressive states that accompany fatigue, see **description of the plant.**

- **Peanut,** generates **Serotonin levels** that the brain interprets as a feeling of well-being, in cases of depression, see **description of the plant.**

- **Perforate St John's-wort,** the infusion acts against depression and associated pathologies. Encapsulated powder can be used, see **description of the plant,** forms of uses **VII (1, 2, 3, 4).**

- **Saffron crocus,** consume for 6 to 8 weeks, as effective as Fluoxetine, always in mild or moderate cases, see **description of the plant.**

- **Siberian ginseng,** it is used to be extremely useful in states of asthenia, **caution,** see **description of the plant.**

- **Spirulina,** effective against depressive fatigue in lung diseases, such as COPD, see **description of the plant.**

- **Turmeric,** stimulates the nervous system with immune effects on mood, causing the production of Serotonin, see **description of the plant.**

- **Vanilla,** deal with depression problems, see **description of the plant.**

- **Yam,** for depression problems, see **description of the plant.**

Detoxifying

- **Ayahuasca,** the Amazonian region in northern Peru became known for its cocaine production, but it is now also due **to the use of medicinal plants** such as Ayahuasca, which local healers use to treat **drug addiction.** And considered "wise" by indigenous people who have been using it for 3000 years. "When Ayahuasca is taken, all perceptions of the senses are amplified: hearing, sight, smell and all internal psychic functions". **It becomes more evident their emotional problems, their family or health** issues and can become aware of elements that escaped ", see **description of the plant.**

- **Azuki red beans,** It is used in **detoxification** treatments, thanks to its contribution in thiamine or vitamin B1, see **description of the plant.**

- **Bitter-wood,** against alcoholism, **consuming in any way** to treat complementary, **precaution,** see **description of the plant.**

- **Blue passionflower,** effective plant for the psychic symptomatology of the **abstinence syndrome** against placebos, valued in **drug addicts opioids** in cure of cessation, and as a **light anxiolytic** without risk of dependence, see **description of the plant,** form of use **VII.**

- **Catnip,** by exerting a relaxing effect, it regulates sleep and eliminates the headaches associated with the abstinence syndrome in addition. It also protects the respiratory system, see **description of the plant.**

- **Common dandelion,** helps to purify the blood, very important **to abandon the habit of alcohol consumption,** see **description of the plant.**

- **Cucumber,** contains a large number of Alanine, Arginine and Glutamine, which have a therapeutic effect, in patients with alcoholic hepatic cirrhosis, see **description of the plant.**

- **Durmast oak,** the essence of the crust causes an **aversion to intoxicating drinks in alcoholics,** see **description of the plant.**

- **English primrose,** the power of your tincture is used to treat alcoholism problems, see **description of the plant.**

- **Evening primrose or Sundrops,** treats alcoholism by relieving **abstinence symptoms** and promoting the normalization of liver enzymes, it also decreases the damage caused to the brain by alcohol, see **description of the plant.**

- **Female ginseng,** its essential oil has managed to modulate the release of dopamine in some areas of the brain. **It is recommended for smoking, alcoholism, or drugs,** see **description of the plant.**

- **Garlic,** against alcoholism consume daily raw in salads or directly (they are sold in Hypermarkets glass jars with garlic in brine, avoiding the halitosis problem), see **description of the plant.**

- **Green coffe,** it has important levels of Levodopa (L-dopa), the precursor of Dopamine, so it is possible that it can increase the levels of neurotransmitters associated with abstinence. Dopamine as such does not exist in the plant kingdom. **It is recommended for addictions such as smoking, alcoholism, or drugs,** see **description of the plant.**

- **Indian fig opuntia,** against alcoholism is used in the form of extracts (follow package directions), see **description of the plant.**

- **Indian gooseberry or Amla,** protects the hepatopancreas from the harmful effects of alcohol, see **description of the plant.**

- **Indian pennywort,** It is very effective as a tonic and nerve regenerator, being sedative in: chronic delirious syndromes, paranoia, schizophrenic psychosis, psychotic disorders, nervous agitation, alcoholic alcohol hallucinosis, manic disturbances and their manifestations, see **description of the plant.**

- **Kava,** the infusion, **only used under facultative control,** has been shown to join sites in the brain associated with **addiction and compulsive desire** due to the supplementation of its substance, Kavapirones, which **decreases the effects of abstinence.** It is recommended for **smoking, alcoholism, drugs** (cocaine, heroin), see **description of the plant.**

- **Kinkeliba,** African plant, recommended to detoxify people addicted to opium, dose **under medical indication,** see **description of the plant.**

- **Kudzu,** it manages to reduce the manifestation of **abstinence symptoms.** The most important active principles are isoflavonoids, Puerarina, Daizina and Daidzein. It also has anxiolytic effects and acts in several ways in the same direction. **It is recommended for smoking, alcoholism, or drugs,** see **description of the plant.**

- **Lice-Bane or Stavesacre,** indispensable because of the **addiction to sex or onamism.** It can heal, **hypochondria and hysteria** that have their starting point in the sexual organs due to libidinous excesses whose consequences are profoundly debilitating, and against the neuroses caused by enervating moral emotions by excitations that start from within, see **description of the plant.**

- **Magnolia-vine,** highly hepatic detoxifying, with two main active components, Schizandrina and Gomisina, which act as protectors against toxic substances such as alcohol, see **description of the plant.**

- **Marsh skullcap,** good for relieving symptoms of abstinence syndrome in **drug addictions, smoking, or medications,** because of their benefits on the nervous system, it alleviates some symptoms of **abstinence syndrome,** see **description of the plant.**

- **Orange flame vine,** American plant, recommended to detoxify persons addicted to opium, **under medical indication,** see **description of the plant.**

- **Perforate St John's-wort,** modulates several neurochemicals, Hyperazine and Hyperforin, the most active compounds. Depression and alcoholism have some neurochemical similarities, such as low serotonin activity in the brain. The extract of Hypericum compared to other antidepressants there are differences. Hypericin has been shown to stimulate the extracellular levels of Dopamine, Noradrenaline and Serotonin, as well as Glutamate, amino acid that excites the brain site responsible **for reactions to panic and stress.** It has been evaluated to stop smoking due to the relationship between smoking and depression when obtaining primary successes. **It is recommended for smoking, alcoholism, or drugs,** see **description of the plant.**

- **Rose,** the infusion is used to combat the annoying effects of alcohol (hangover), it also calms anxiety and alleviates feelings of jealousy and resentment, see **description of the plant.**

- **Rosemary,** it tones the heart and is good tonic that helps to restore energies and to favor the will power, see **description of the plant,** forms of use **VII (1, 2** and **3).**

- **Seneca snakeroot,** tea is very suitable for nasal congestion problems that can come from alcohol, **caution,** see **description of the plant.**

- **Small-leaved lime,** as an anxiolytic, in the face of a mild and sudden state of anxiety, a punctual moment of nervousness or when there is a slight effect of accumulated stress, see **description of the plant.**

- **Southern magnolia,** for the stimulation of the lymphatic system that increases the level of toxins and is eliminated from the body. Reduction of fat accumulation around the liver due to liver failure due to excessive alcohol consumption, called ALD, see **description of plant.**

- **Tamarind,** it is a good remedy for excesses of alcohol and against hangovers, see **description of the plant.**

- **Tick-trefoil,** the most effective **method to combat alcoholism,** causing liver disorders and elevated transaminases, see **description of the plant.**

- **Valerian,** it is recommended for **persons addicted to alcohol or drugs, to mitigate the abstinence syndrome,** see **description of the plant.**

- **West Indian cherry,** fruit very advisable for persons who are leaving an addiction, such as smoking or drinking, their properties are not limited to vitamin C, see **description of the plant.**

Fibromyalgia

Fibromyalgia is a rheumatological disease that is characterized by chronic pain generalized for more than three months. Normally the patient locates this pain in the locomotor system, fatigue, memory problems and changes in moods. Rheumatological disease that mainly affects women, **without a specific medication for the cure of Fibromyalgia.** This book provides specific plants that can have a relief effect to this ailment, also some of the offered could alleviate, in part, these pains.

- **Blue passionflower,** is adequate even in neuralgia, see **description of the plant,** form of use **VII.**

- **Bogbean or Buckbean,** for muscle pain and Fibromyalgia, also combines with other plants such as Silver birch and Celery, see **description of the plant.**

- **Camphor tree,** limited its use for joint pain and rheumatism, diluting a few drops of Camphor oil with olive oil or soap, helps to lessen and reduce inflammation of the pain, see **descriptions of the plants.**

- **Chili pepper,** pain reliever. A single injection of Capsaicin combats certain types of chronic pain for several weeks, see **description of plant.**

- **Evening primrose or Sundrops,** treats post viral syndrome that causes **dizziness due to Fibromyalgia,** see **description of the plant.**

- **Jamaican dogwood,** it is used as an analgesic for neuralgia **or chronic pain,** see **description of the plant.**

- **Lavender,** as a frequent tonic it can help in **conditions of fatigue.** Water cloths of their flowers reduce pain levels, the smell of Lavender can reduce headaches, see **description of the plant.**

- **Mistletoe,** potent analgesic and very effective to combat fibromyalgia or chronic muscle pain, see **description of the plant.**

- **Quinine,** in infusion or 1 dram a day (**adults only**, only one is enough for good results), for neuralgia, see **description of the plant.**

- **Soursop,** counteracts headaches and muscle pain, see **description of the plant.**

- **Vanilla,** helps to control and treat pain due to its analgesic properties, in particular chronic pain of unknown origin, such as Fibromyalgia, see **description of the plant.**

- **White mustard,** effective sedative that acts as an analgesic in the treatment of chronic pain, see **description of the plant.**

Headaches

The plants, **Maca, Blue passionflower, Estragon, Lavender, Lice-Bane or Stavesacre, West Indian cherry,** plants used as headaches are included **in the Stress section.**

- **Aloe vera**, relieves headache, especially that caused by sinusitis, rubbing your inner gel at the temples or chewing, see **description of plant.**

- **Apple,** good in headaches, see **description of the plant.**

- **Asafoetida,** against **headaches and migraines,** dissolve a little in water and drink, see **description of the plant.**

- **Bloodroot,** against headache, **caution,** see **description of the plant,** form of use **VII.**

- **Chestnut fruit,** its consumption brings us closer to eliminating headaches naturally, without resorting to an analgesic, see **description of the plant.**

- **Chicory,** in infusion it is good for treat headaches, see **description of the plant,** form of use **VII.**

- **Cloves,** the flavonoid in infusion alleviates headache, see **description of the plant,** form of use **IV.**

- **Common lady's mantle,** analgesic to combat headaches, **caution,** see **description of the plant.**

- **Copalchi,** using the infusion of its crust serves as an analgesic, **caution,** in reasonable doses is little toxic, **follow indications of medical personnel,** see **description of the plant.**

- **Cowslip primrose,** use as an analgesic against headaches, see **description of the plant**, form of use **VII.**

- **Devil's Claw,** in infusion it is analgesic and highly effective for headaches, see **description of the plant,** form of use **VII.**

- **Eastern teaberry,** your essential oil can help alleviate headache by rubbing your temples a bit, see **description of the plant.**

- **Guarana,** it produces a state of tranquility despite its caffeine, personsuse it to alleviate headaches, see **description of the plant.**

- **Henna,** mix flowers from the plant with a little vinegar and apply over the forehead and temples, alleviate the discomfort, see **description plant.**

- **Herb Bennet,** the leaves and roots in infusion combat the headache, see **description of the plant,** form of use **VII (2).**

- **Horseradish,** for headache (cataplasm on the nape), see **description of the plant,** form of use **IV.**

- **Ice-cream-bean,** its intake calm the headache, see **description plant.**

- **Jamaican dogwood,** it is used as a weak analgesic, it has an advantage over opium that it does not produce heaviness, see **description of plant.**

- **Luma chequen,** their yolks in decoction thrown in the baths mitigate all kinds of pains, to see **description of the plant.**

- **Meridian fennel,** eliminates or mitigates the headache, through dressings on the forehead with an infusion, see **description of the plant.**

- **Mint,** the antiseptic and antiviral effect of its extract for its content in polyphenols, is an effective remedy and consists of applying to the affected area (forehead and temples), see **description of the plant.**

- **Neroli oil,** applying a few drops on a hot or cold compress, relieves headaches and neuralgia, see **description of the plant.**

- **Orange,** its consumption is useful in some cases of headaches caused by excess toxins in the body. Infusion (husk/peel) soothes headaches caused by stress, see **description of the plant.**

- **Primrose,** the root contains substances related to acetyl salicylic acid, which provide analgesic properties to calm headaches, see **description of the plant,** form of use **VII.**

- **Psoralea or Otholobium,** in infusion against headache, see **description of the plant,** form of use **VII.**

- **Quinine,** in infusion or 1 dram per day (**only adults,** only one is enough for good results), for neuralgia and headache, see **description of the plant.**

- **Small-leaved lime,** it acts as a relaxant; infusion is ideal to improve symptoms such as **headaches or migraines,** take **only as a side effect of digestive discomfort,** see **description of the plant.**

- **Soursop,** counteracts headaches and muscle pain, see **description of the plant.**

- **Verdolaga,** as an analgesic, drink the juice of the plant or mix with oil and apply as a poultice on the head, see **description of the plant.**

- **Vervain,** as an analgesic acts against headache, ingested or in topical use, see **description of the plant**, forms of use **VII (1 and 3).**

- **Viper's bugloss or Blueweed,** In some parts of Europe the infusion has been used for the treatment of headache, see **description of the plant.**

- **Weeping paperbark,** in **inhalations** its analgesic properties are useful in headaches that usually accompany colds, see **description of the plant.**

- **White mustard,** its use is a quite effective sedative for headaches, see **description of the plant.**

- **White willow,** infusion or capsules may help alleviate the headache associated with nervous tension, see **description of the plant.**

- **Yam,** against the usual headaches, see **description of the plant.**

- **Finally,** we describe the plants that only **the simple infusion is necessary to ingest,** in this case **against the headaches:**
Ajuga iva, Catnip, Cumin, Devil's backbone, Dill, Garden angelica, Helychrysum, Jasmine, Kava, Kudzu, Large-leaved lime, Lemon verbena, Marjoram, Marsh skullcap, Mexican pepperleaf, Olive, Red tea, Tamarind, Tansy, ...Continúe
... **Thyme, Vanilla, Vitex or Chaste tree, Wild mint or Corn mint, Yellow trumpetbush, Yerba mate.**

The **plants can be potentiated** with others for the same ailment, but it is **always convenient to remember,** the perfect use of each plant according **to its description,** in case there is any **interaction with drugs or possible contraindications.**

Insomnia

To recover lost sleep habits, before resorting to pills or other remedies **it is recommended to have a ritual that your body identifies as the rest route. For example,** always disconnect at the same time from electronic devices (telephone, tables, TV, etc.); showering before bedtime to relax, eat lightly during dinner, go out for a walk in the evenings, etc.

The plants, **Narrow-leaf strap fern, Soursop, West Indian cherry,** plants used as insomnia are included **in the Stress section.**

- **Artichoke,** its consumption combats insomnia, see **description of the plant,** form of consume **VIII.**

- **Ashwagandha or Indian ginseng,** taking it at night it helps to sleep better, see **description of the plant**, form of use **VII.**

- **Baikal skullcap,** the infusion of 3 or 4 sprigs of fresh, in a cup before going to bed, insomnia, see **description of the plant.**

- **Bitter orange,** with the flowers the orange blossom water is prepared, which is used as a sedative to facilitate sleep, see **description of the plant.**

- **Blue passionflower,** one of the most reputable plants as a remedy for its somnolent action, with the virtue of causing a dream very similar to physiological and a quick awakening, complete, without consequences of depression, prostration or psychic bewilderment, see **description of the plant,** form of use **VII.**

- **Boldo,** the infusion fights insomnia as excellent relaxing. Take a small cup before you go to bed, **caution,** see **description of the plant.**

- **Briar root,** as a sedative helps persons with mild insomnia, see **description of the plant.**

- **Butterbur,** the infusion is used to fight insomnia, **caution,** see **description of the plant.**

- **Calamintha,** take **1 drop of the essence, orally,** before you go to bed to combat insomnia, see **description of the plant.**

- **Catnip,** the infusion has never ceased to be used, especially against insomnia, see **description of the plant.**

- **Cherry,** one of the few food sources containing Melatonin, antioxidant, helps regulate sleep cycles, see **description of the plant.**

- **Chickpea,** its high content in Magnesium, Phosphorus and vitamins of group B, its consumption is adequate in situations of lack of sleep, **description of the plant.**

- **Chicory,** unlike coffee, it is used to combat somnolence states, see **description of the plant,** form of use **VII.**

- **Chinese wolfberry,** it serves **to regulate sleep,** see **description plant.**

- **Cinnamon with honey,** take a spoonful with a glass of warm water before going to bed, see **description of the plant and Honey.**

- **Common hawthorn or Single-seeded hawthorn,** the flowers are excellent for insomnia and against neurovegetative imbalances. Make a tisane with a handful of its flowers in boiling water. Rest, strain and drink, a cup at lunch and another at dinner, see **description of the plant.**

- **Cowslip primrose,** it is very useful against insomnia, see **description of the plant,** form of use **VII.**

- **Cucumber,** contains large amounts of vitamin B1, with a good effect of calming the nerves and treating insomnia, see **description of the plant.**

- **English primrose,** tincture is applied for insomnia, see **description of the plant.**

- **Estragon or Tarragon,** a teaspoon dry per cup of water in infusion **(you can drink at your discretion),** or add fresh and finely chopped to your meals, see **description of the plant.**

- **Fennel,** the gargles of Fennel, Mint, Sage and Valerian, against the blockage of the throat that causes sleep apnea, see **descriptions of plants.**

- **Garden angelica,** infusion of leaves is used in sleep disorders and insomnia, see **description of the plant**.

- **Garden nasturtium,** mixed in the salads, leaves and fresh flowers by the night, facilitate sleep, see **description of the plant.**

- **Grape vine,** boil their dried leaves, infused, with a teaspoon of dessert per cup of water for 10 minutes. Rest 10 minutes and take every ¼ hour 1 tablespoon, as a sedative is used in insomnia, see **description of the plant.**

- **Grenadia or Sweet granadilla,** it´s relaxant, favors the sleep of persons who suffer from insomnia, see **description of the plant.**

- **Honeysuckles,** the tea of its white flowers acts against insomnia, see **description of the plant.**

- **Indian sandalwood,** to improve the quality of sleep, see **description of the plant.**

- **Japanese pagoda tree,** is used against insomnia, **precaution with dose**, see **description of the plant.**

- **Kava,** the infusion, **under facultative control**, is used to treat insomnia, in adequate doses, **caution**, see **description of the plant.**

- **Large-leaved lime,** like the Valerian, it favors the night rest, helps to conciliate the sleep, reduces the states of nervousness that prevent sleeping. An infusion before bed is one of the most effective natural remedies against insomnia, and as a soothing nervous system also makes it a remedy, see **description of the plant.**

- **Large-leaved linden,** before going to bed the infusion has antispasmodic effects, acting against insomnia, see **description of the plant,** form of use **VII.**

- **Lavender,** it has properties that help persons to fall asleep and deeply, it is recommended to use Lavender oil in cases of insomnia (before prescribing sleeping pills). If it does not work, with the prescription of any drug, it can be used simultaneously to fall asleep, see **description of plant.**

- **Lemon balm or Melissa,** being slightly hypnotic and sedative, it acts against sleep disturbances, see **description of the plant.**

- **Lemon verbena,** in infusion is effective to treat insomnia, see **description of the plant.**

- **Lettuce,** helps calm the nervous system and insomnia a glass of lettuce juice helps you sleep better, see **description of the plant.**

- **Lúpulo,** beneficial in persons who suffer or are attacked by insomnia and can not get to sleep, see **description of the plant,** form of use **VII.**

- **Maca,** its consumption benefits sleep by making it deeper, see **description of the plant.**

- **Magnolia-vine,** fruit helps to improve sleep, see **description of plant.**

- **Marjoram,** is used against insomnia, see **description of the plant.**

- **Marsh skullcap,** it is used to improve insomnia by helping to rest in the absence of sleep, see **description of the plant.**

- **Mint,** see **in Fennel,** see **descriptions of the plants.**

- **Naranjilla,** effective in promoting sleep, see **description of the plant.**

- **Nutmeg,** help your consumption to overcome insomnia, including massage with your essential oil before bedtime, see **description of plant.**

- **Parsnip,** consume against insomnia, see **description of the plant.**

- **Pennyroyal or Pennyrile,** an infusion is excellent to relax the body, to fight the problems to sleep, to see **description of the plant.**

- **Perforate St John's-wort or Hyperucum,** boil 3 minutes, stand 5 minutes, strain and drink 2 to 3 cups daily, there is also encapsulated powder, see **description of the plant.**

- **Potato,** contains Choline, very important and versatile nutrient of potatoes, helping to reconcile sleep, see **description of the plant.**

- **Primrose,** plant that is traditionally used against insomnia, see **description of the plant**, form of use **VII.**

- **Pumpkin,** a decoction of their crushed pipes, without shells, in water or milk is used against insomnia, see **description of the plant.**

- **Red clover,** for insomnia the infusion is taken 1 hour before going to sleep, see **description of the plant.**

- **Red pepper,** contains **vitamin B6** and **Magnesium,** combination that reduces insomnia, see **description of the plant.**

- **Reishi mushroom,** to treat insomnia, **caution,** see **description plant.**

- **Rooibos,** for its relaxing qualities, **it helps us sleep better at night. Does not contain Theine, in case of insomnia,** it is an infusion that gives us Magnesium, an essential nutrient that helps us relax our muscles, see **description of the plant.**

- **Sage or Garden sage,** see **in Fennel,** see **descriptions of the plants.**

- **Senecio oreophyton,** a tisane every night, induces a restful and quiet sleep, see **description of the plant,** form of use **VII.**

- **Small-leaved lime,** good ally to recover or create good sleep habits. Take at least one hour before the set time to sleep, ensure that it is always the same time its relaxing property of the nervous system induces sleep, its action is mild. Therefore, it is ideal for when you have an isolated case of lack of sleep, see **description of the plant.**

- **Spearmint,** of sedative properties, being used in insomnia problems in infusions, **caution,** see **description of the plant.**

- **Spirulina,** it has a high content of melatonin so it is indicated for insomnia, see **description of the plant.**

- **Sweet flag or Calamus,** the decoction of the rhizome is excellent, take a bath persons suffering from insomnia problems, see **description of plant.**

- **Sweetscented bedstraw,** soothing of proven effects, the infusion is considered a good sedative and hypnotic, in situations of insomnia, take immediately before going to bed, see **see description of the plant,** form of use it **VII.**

- **Tansy,** the infusion, in scientific studies has been shown to be an effective method to improve sleep, see **description of the plant.**

- **Valerian,** see **in Fennel,** see **descriptions of the plants.**

- **Vanilla,** helps insomnia problems like sedative, see **description of plant.**

- **Virginia water horehound,** against insomnia, see **description plant.**

- **Water lilies or Nymphaea,** infusions of seeds or a root, help to get rid of some problems of the central nervous system against insomnia. The extract improves sleep, see **description of the plant.**

- **Withania aristata,** used the infusion of the root crust is sedative and narcotic in case of insomnia, **caution,** see **description of the plant.**

- **Wood violet,** is used to combat insomnia, see **description of the plant,** form of use **VII.**

- **Yam,** to treat insomnia, see **description of the plant.**

- **Ylang Ylang,** It serves to relax in situations of bad dreams, **caution,** see **description of the plant.**

Migraines

- **Asafoetida,** migraine has become a part of our current life, dissolve some Asafoetida in water and drink, see **description of the plant.**

- **Banana,** next to the tree Tomato (Tamarillo), it is considered as one of the fruits that contributes to cure migraines and severe headaches. For 10 days, 1 ½ h. before breakfast, eat a well-ripe Banana with a glass of water. Starting on the 11th, drink Tamarillo juice in water until day 20. Repeat twice, see **descriptions of plants.**

- **Bitter kola,** its oil (Argan Web) is recommended to alleviate the symptoms of migraine. **Important to consult a specialist before using,** see **description of the plant.**

- **Bloodroot,** ideal against migraines, **caution,** see **description of the plant,** form of use **VII.**

- **Blue passionflower,** is suitable for migraines, even in neuralgia, see **description of the plant,** form of use **VII.**

- **Broad-leaved paperbark,** mix with some base vegetable oil and massage the nape or temples in case of migraines, see **description of plant.**

- **Cassava or Yuca,** the powerful properties of the roots are anti-inflammatory, help in the treatment of general pain associated with migraine, see **description of the plant.**

- **Cowslip primrose,** It is useful to treat migraine problems, see **description of the plant,** form of use **VII.**

- **Daysy,** combat migraines, **caution,** see **description of the plant.**

- **Ginger,** inhibits the effects of Prostaglandin, the substance that causes inflammation the blood vessels in the brain to swell, infuse, see **description of the plant.**

- **Gingko,** linfusion is used for episodes of severe migraine, see **description of the plant.**

- **Kava,** the infusion, **under facultative control,** is used for attention deficit, and migraines, **caution,** see **description of the plant.**

- **Kudzu,** interesting in case of migraines, see **description of the plant.**

- **Large-leaved linden,** is used in infusion to relieve migraines, see **description of the plant,** form of use **VII.**

- **Lovage,** is used against the Hemicrania (disorder characterized by daily, chronic and limited migraine attacks on one side of the head that do not extend to the other), see **description of the plant.**

- **Mint,** the antiseptic and antiviral effect that has its origin in the content of Polyphenols, make the extract an effective remedy against migraines by applying the essential oil to the affected area (forehead and temples), see **description of the plant.**

- **Perforate St John's-wort,** normal infusion, boil 3 minutes, stand 5 minutes, strain and drink 2 to 3 cups daily. Also encapsulated powder for migraines, see **description of the plant.**

- **Small-leaved lime,** acts as a relaxant, the infusion, **only as a side effect of digestive discomfort,** is ideal to improve symptoms such as headaches or migraines, see **description of the plant.**

- **Tamarillo or Tomato tree,** considered as one of the fruits that contributes to cure migraines and severe headaches, **see in Banana,** see **description of the plant.**

- **Tansy,** Scientific studies have shown that it is effective against migraines. Boil in 300 ml of water with 5 gr. of leaves, 10 minutes. Cover and stand, take daily for a week and rest two, and again take another week and so on. Also boil in a liter of water 50 gr. of flowrs and ...**Continue**

... stalks 10 minutes. Cover and rest, soak a cloth, apply on the forehead and leave to relieve, see **description of the plant.**

- **Vervain,** is used against migraines, see **description of the plant**, form of use **VII (3).**

- **West Indian cherry,** of analgesic and anti-inflammatory properties, due to anthocyanins, a quality that helps to cure migraines, such as Aspirin and Ibuprofen, see **description of the plant.**

- **White willow,** in infusion or capsules can help alleviate migraine headaches, see **description of the plant.**

- **Wood violet,** the infusions and decoctions relieve migraines, see **description of the plant,** form of use **VII.**

- **Yam,** against the usual headaches and migraines, see **description plant.**

- **Finally,** we describe the plants that only **the simple infusion is necessary to ingest,** in this case against chronic headaches or migraines:
Bogbean or Buckbean, Butterbur, Common lady's mantle, Garden angelica, Large-leaved lime, Lemon balm or Melissa, Marsh skullcap.
The **plants can be potentiated** with others for the same ailment, but it is **always convenient to remember,** the perfect use of each plant according **to its description,** in case there is any **interaction with drugs or possible contraindications.**

Sedatives

- **Ajuga iva,** the infusion is beneficial in case of diseases of the nervous system in general, see **description of the plant.**

- **Artichoke,** consume for nervousness, see **description of the plant,** form of consume **VIII**

- **Asafoetida,** help against nervous diseases such as **hysteria, seizures, syncope** and other disorders, see **description of the plant.**

- **Ashwagandha,** having a sedative effect acts on the central nervous system, see **description of the plant,** form of use **VII.**

- **Ayahuasca,** it serves as a sedative for the treatment of Parkinson's, has great qualities such as sedative and narcotic, **used moderately** can combat various conditions, including abstinence from cocaine, see **description of the plant,** form of use **VII.**

- **Banana,** for their vitamin B content, they are very good to calm the nervous system, do not hesitate to eat Bananas as a snack, see **description of the plant.**

- **Bitter lettuce,** crush the stems of the Lettuce and then squeeze the juice through a canvas. It is allowed to curdle in the sun. Dosage of 5 to 10 gr. When you want to calm a **state of excitability, caution,** see **description of the plant.**

- **Black henbane,** the alkaloids of this plant give excellent properties as a sedative, **should be used with extreme caution, and only under medical prescription,** see **description of the plant.**

- **Black sesame,** its oil is very rich in Magnesium, as a **strengthening of the nervous system, use with caution,** see **description of the plant**

- **Blackcurrant,** the berries are rich in B vitamins, and in Magnesium, **very beneficial for the nervous system,** see **description of the plant.**

- **Blue passionflower,** ideal for persons under nervous tension, see **description of the plant,** form of use **VII.**

- **Boldo,** the infusion is an excellent relaxing. Take a small cup before sleep, **caution,** see **description of the plant.**

- **Borage,** the infusion regulates nervous disorders and the essential oil favors the functioning of the nervous system, see **description of the plant, form of use VII.**

- **Briar root,** it is used as a sedative helping to **calm nervous states,** stress, anxiety, see **description of the plant.**

- **Butterbur,** the infusion is used in nervous disorders, **caution,** see **description of the plant.**

- **Cacao or Cocoa,** stimulates the nervous system, see **description plant.**

- **Calamintha,** take **only 1 drop of the essence, orally, as a sedative,** against insomnia or stress, see **description of the plant,** form of use **VII.**

- **Catnip,** the infusion against nervousness, see **description of the plant.**

- **Cecropia,** the infusion, as a sedative and spasmodic, **calms the palpitations** and nervous disorders, see **description plant,** form of use **VII.**

- **Chickpea,** its high content of Magnesium, Phosphorus and vitamins of group B, are suitable in nervous situations, see **description of the plant.**

- **Chicory,** in infusion, a cup before dinner calms states of nervousness, see **description of the plant,** form of use **VII.**

- **Cissampelos pareira,** useful in case of mental disorders, **epilepsy, delirium, convulsions, caution,** see **description of the plant.**

- **Cistus or Rockrose,** its notable for its sedative action of the nervous system, in infusion, caution, see **description of the plant**, form of use **VII.**

- **Clary or Clary sage,** is used for nervousness, mix and use as a fragrance or inhale from the bottle, as required, see **description of the plant,** form of use **VII (2).**

- **Coffe,** its consumption could protect the Parkinson's in some cases, see **description of the plant.**

- **Common hawthorn,** the flowers are excellent as a sedative, the tisane is made with a handful of flowers in boiling water. Cool, strain and sip one cup at lunch and another at dinner. This medication does not present any danger and can be prolonged as much as you want, see **description plant.**

- **Common poppy,** the infusion of **the seeds brings benefits** for its content in certain alkaloids that help to **calm the nerves,** and at the time to relaxing our nervous system.   Regular and daily consumption of Poppy seeds are especially recommended in situations of stress and sleep problems, acting as **a sedative,** see **description of the plant,** form of consume **VIII.**

- **Common soapwort,** it is used for **hysteria, epilepsy, caution,** see **description of the plant.**

- **Corydalis cava,** as a nervous sedative, **caution,** as a complementary treatment to Parkinson's disease, see **description of the plant.**

- **Cowslip primrose,** help in neuralgia disorders, see **description of the plant,** form of use **VII.**

- **Cucumber,** with large amount of vitamin B1, it is beneficial to improve the nervous system with good calming effect, see **description of the plant.**

- **Edging lobelia,** it acts as a nervous tonic when sedative and narcotic, it is considered one of the most effective systemic relaxants. Offers an integral combination of stimulation and relaxation to treat inflammation and **seizure disorders such as:** epilepsy, hysterical convulsions, precaution, see **description of the plant.**

- **Elms,** its used in infusion as a good painkiller, see **description of the plant,** form of use **VII.**

- **English primrose,** it is used its tincture is applied in diseases of the nervous system, see **description of the plant.**

- **Escarole,** its high content of vitamin C, and Potassium exerts a positive influence on the central nervous system, see **description of the plant.**

- **Estragon or Tarragon,** it is sedative by taking a teaspoon of Estragon, dry, per cup of water infused (can be taken at discretion) or add it fresh and finely chopped to meals, see **description of the plant.**

- **Evening primrose or Sundrops,** effective in psychiatric problems such as: **schizophrenia and dementia** caused by old age, see **description of the plant.**

- **Evergreen oak,** as a sedative it helps **decrease nervous tics, convulsions** and stress symptoms, see **description of the plant.**

- **Fragrant incense,** used with Lavender relaxes and calms, **only burned,** see **description of the plant.**

- **Garden angelica,** infusion of leaves acts as an analgesic in **nerve disorders**, see **description of the plant.**

- **Garlic,** the consumption of 4 garlic a day helps reduce anxiety and nerves, **caution,** see **description of the plant.**

- **Geen pepper,** its content in Magnesium is good for the functioning of the nerves, see **description of the plant.**

- **Grape vine,** the leaves in infusion are made with a dessert teaspoon of dried leaves per cup of water, for 10 minutes. Rest 10 minutes and take a spoonful every ¼ h., as a sedative is used in nervous states and **hyperexcitation, neurasthenia, neurosis,** see **description of the plant.**

- **Great mullein or Mullein,** consumed as tea you can get relaxation, for its slight sedative effect, see **description of the plant,** form of use **VII.**

- **Green tea,** its properties can be used to help in the treatment of Parkinson's, see **description of the plant.**

- **Grenadia,** used as a natural tranquilizer, its consumption is recommended for the stabilization of the nerves, see **description of plant.**

- **Ground elder,** the infusion is sedative, see **description of the plant.**

- **Guarana,** it produces a state of tranquility, despite having a lot of caffeine, it is used to alleviate all kinds of pain, see **description of the plant.**

- **Guatemalan indigo plant,** it has been proven the effectiveness as antiepileptic, depressant of the central nervous system, and antibiotic, **caution,** see **description of the plant.**

- **Hazelnut,** useful for the nervous system, and necessary for the creation of Myelin that increases the efficiency of nerve impulses, see **description of the plant.**

- **Heliotropium,** the root is valued by its relaxing properties, **caution,** see **description of the plant,** form of use **VII.**

- **Hop,** among its properties, its relaxing and sedative action stands out, see **description of the plant,** form of use **VII.**

- **Indian lotus or Lotus,** the infusion is used as a relaxant, see **description of the plant.**

- **Indian pennywort,** its use is very effective as a tonic and regenerator of the nerves, **being of sedative action in:** chronic delusional syndromes, paranoia, schizophrenic psychosis, psychotic disorders, nervous agitation, alcoholic hallucinosis, manic disorders and their manifestations, see **description of the plant.**

- **Indian sandalwood,** the aroma of sandalwood improves breathing, promotes meditation and creativity, **calms feelings of panic,** see **description of the plant.**

- **Ivy,** the leaves as anti neuralgic, see **description of the plant.**

- **Jamaican dogwood,** it is used as a sedative of the nervous system, it has an advantage over opium, by not producing heaviness, see **description of the plant.**

- **Jasmine,** studies have shown that the scent of Jasmine can **produce a soothing effect** that serene senses, see **description of the plant.**

- **Kalonchoe,** It is used for psychological illnesses: **schizophrenia, panic attacks and fears,** see **description of the plant.**

- **Kava,** to use the infusion **under facultative control,** being its most important property to relax and induce tranquility in the altered nerves and, against hyperactivity (ADHD), epilepsy, psychosis, **caution,** see **description of the plant.**

- **Kudzu,** it is recommended to use as a parasympathetic nervous system relaxant, see **description of the plant.**

- **Large-leaved lime,** of sedative effect, it can cause drowsiness in some people but it is not the usual, because its action is not so potent as to interfere in the daily life, to see **description of the plant.**

- **Large-leaved linden,** in infusion is used against **spasms,** insomnia, **hysteria, hypochondriasis,** nerves, as sedative and slightly hypnotic, take before bedtime, see **description of the plant,** form of use **VII.**

- **Lavender,** as a tonic it can help in conditions of the nervous system also the Lavender Sandalwood. The oil in topical use helps in several **problems** related **to dementia,** see **description of the plant.**

- **Lemon balm or Melissa,** it is slightly hypnotic and sedative, good for combating nervous conditions, **hyperactivity, irritability,** see **description of the plant.**

- **Lemon verbena,** in infusion is used to relax and tone the nerves, see **description of the plant.**

- **Lice-Bane or Stavesacre,** indispensable because of the **addiction to sex or onamism.** It can heal, **hypochondria and hysteria** that have their starting point in the sexual organs due to libidinous excesses whose consequences are profoundly debilitating, and against the neuroses caused by enervating moral emotions by excitations that start from within, **caution,** see **description of the plant.**

- **Maca,** for essential bodily and metabolic **functions such as:** the physiology of the nervous system. Of analgesic effect thanks to the Terpenoids and Saponins that act as a sedative, see **description of plant.**

- **Marjoram,** it is mildly sedative for nervous excitement, take a small spoonful of Marjoram per cup, 3 times or more a day, see **description of the plant.**

- **Marsh labrador tea,** it is used as a sedative, being narcotic **only under medical supervision,** see **description of the plant.**

- **Marsh skullcap,** alleviates dementia for its benefits on the nervous system, see **description of the plant.**

- **Marsh skullcap,** infusion of 3 or 4 sprigs of fresh, three times a day, is good for **nervous exhaustion and excitability,** see **description of the plant.**

- **Martagon lily,** infused flowers and bulbs are effective as a sedative in diseases and disorders of the nervous system, see **description of the plant.**

- **Mignonette tree,** the leaves and flowers, macerated in wine is used **against hysteria**, 1 little glass every day, see **description of the plant.**

- **Mint,** it has a vasoconstrictor and vasodilator effect, acting as an anesthetic, applied on the skin generates a sensation of relaxation, see **description of the plant.**

- **Motherwort,** in infusion it is attributed a sedative action superior to Valerian, see **description of the plant,** form of use **VII.**

- **Muira puama,** deals with nervous system disorders, see **description of the plant.**

- **Muskmelon or Melon,** eating **only melon for 24 hours** or, having **breakfast melon for a week** you can clean the body helping to reduce the nerves, see **description of the plant.**

- **Myrtle,** it is used as a sedative for its compounds, see **description of the plant,** form of use **VII.**

- **Myrrh,** in infusión as a sedative, relax and improve the rest, see **description of the plant.**

- **Narrow-leaf strap fern,** for nervous disorders, insomnia and stress, in infusions or as drinking water regularly, see **description of the plant,** form of use **VII.**

- **Nut,** its consumption **nourishes the nervous system** and maintains its functions in good condition, see **description of the plant.**

- **Nutmeg,** in the meals sprinkled or massage with its essential oil, it is effective as a tranquilizer, and helps to induce sleep, see **description plant.**

- **Orange,** infusion provides a solution **in cases of epilepsy and situations of hysteria,** see **description of the plant.**

- **Oregano,** as a sedative it can help in the prevention of Parkinson's disease, see **description of the plant,** form of use **VII.**

- **Pea,** its type B vitamins, make it essential for the correct functioning of the nervous system, see **description of the plant.**

- **Peach,** recommended to treat cases of neurosis, for having the ability to **protect nerve cells,** see **description of the plant.**

- **Pennyroyal or Pennyrile,** its **sedative properties** make it an excellent infusion to relax the body and combat symptoms of nervousness, see **description of the plant.**

- **Perforate St John's-wort or Hypericum,** normal infusion, boil 3 minutes, stand 5 minutes, strain and drink 2 to 3 cups daily. Also powder encapsulated as a sedative, see **description of the plant.**

- **Perilla or Deulkkae,** decreases **aggression, violence,** see **description of the plant.**

- **Pineapple mint,** in infusion it is effective as a sedative, see **description of the plant.**

- **Pistachio,** it favors the functions of the nervous system by playing a crucial role in the formation of the Myelin in the insulating sheath. It also favors the synthesis of Serotonin, Melatonin, Epinephrine and Gamma-Aminobutyric Acid (GABA), an amino acid that induces the calmof the nervous system, see **description of the plant.**

- **Pollen,** it is efficient in counteracting situations of psychic exhaustion, for its toning and stimulating effect in regulating the nervous system, see **description of Pollen,** form of consume **VIII.**

- **Primrose,** has properties that calm and regularize the nervous activity, see **description of the plant,** form of use **VII.**

- **Quince,** It is used to combat the problems and diseases of the nervous system, see **description of the plant.**

- **Red clover,** useful in the treatment of nerves, see **description of plant.**

- **Rice,** its consumption balances the nervous system, see **description of the plant.**

- **Rooibos,** before much nervousness **relaxes our body and our mind,** see description of the plant.

- **Rose,** the infusion reduces nervous tension, calms emotions and relieves **feelings of regret, jealousy and resentment,** see **description of the plant.**

- **Rue or Herb-of-grace,** can help to relax having a soothing effect on the nervous system, **caution,** see **description of the plant.**

- **Safflower or Hua Hong,** as a sedative is used to treat **cases of hysteria that are related to Chlorosis,** see **description of the plant.**

- **Saffron crocus,** supplement for those who suffer from nerves. Due to its sedative and aromatic substances, it helps to fight anxiety and nervousness, see **description of the plant.**

- **Saturn peaches,** helps to prevent states from nervousness, see **description of the plant.**

- **Seneca snakeroot,** the infusion is used to attenuate **the heart palpitations** of nervous origin, **caution,** see **description of the plant.**

- **Senecio oreophyton**, of very marked action in all **diseases of nervous origin**, see **description of the plant,** form of use **VII.**

- **Silver wattle or Mimosa,** its soothing and nerve-reducing, see **description of the plant.**

- **Soursop,** the chewed leaves, have a high sedative power, serves to **calm nerves** and stress, see **description of the plant.**

- **Sumatra benzoin tree,** it is used as a soothing and sedative internally or externally in: ointments, soaps, tinctures, essential oil, see **description of the plant.**

- **Sumbal or Muskroot,** good sedative for the **hysteria**, see **description of the plant.**

- **Sunflower,** among its components, thiamine (vitamin B1) allows to avoid **nervous system problems and chronic fatigue,** see **description of the plant**

- **Sweet flag or Calamus,** the decoction of the rhizome is excellent for taking a bath, persons who suffer from sleep problems, and **very useful for nerves**, see **description of the plant,** form of use **VII.**

- **Sweetscented bedstraw,** in infusion, it is a good sedative and hypnotic as a soothing, with proven effects, it can be used in situations of nervousness, **advisable to use only elderly persons,** see **description of the plant,** form of use **VII.**

- **Tea of Aragon or Rock tea,** the infusion is an excellent nervous tonifier, as it does not contain Thein, it has a sedative and relaxing effect, see **description of the plant.**

- **Vachellia aroma or Aromita,** tea has sedative properties for multiple ailments, see **description of the plant.**

- **Valerian,** it is used as a sedative and relaxing, **reducing nervousness and agitation,** see **description of the plant.**

- **Vanilla,** of soothing and sedative effects, see **description of the plant.**

- **Vervain,** it is used as a sedative, see **description of the plant**, form of use **VII (2).**

- **Vetiver,** as a sedative in infusion, serving to relax and calm situations of strong tensions, see **description of the plant.**

- **Water lilies or Nymphaea,** with the seeds it is possible to eliminate some problems of the central nervous system. They are frequently recommended for the fight against more frequent events and excessive psychological loads. The oil is widely used for nervous tension, see **description of the plant.**

- **White horehound,** infusion is used for nervous disorders, see **description of the plant.**

- **White mustard,** effective in the treatment of Neuralgia, see **description of the plant.**

- **Wild mint or Corn mint,** effective to treat nervous tension, see **description of the plant.**

- **Withania aristata,** infusion of root crust, as sedative and narcotic is used **against trigeminal neuralgia, caution,** see **description of the plant.**

- **Wood violet,** as a sedative relieves nervous tension, stress and **hysteria,** see **description of the plant,** form of use **VII.**

- **Yam,** for irritability, mood changes, see **description of the plant.**

- **Yellow jessamine or Carolina jasmine,** It is used for the nervous system, see **description of the plant**

- **Yellow pepper,** it is used to improve the functioning of the nervous system, see **description of the plant.**

- **Yellow trumpetbush,** of analgesic properties, acts as a soothing and intense sedative to relax nervous alterations, see **description of the plant.**

- **Ylang Ylang,** through massage, relax in situations of stress, **panic,** bad dreams, **excessive shyness,** nervous attacks, **feelings of anger**, tension and nervous **irritability, caution,** see **description of the plant.**

Sick headache

- **Broad-leaved paperbark,** mixed with some base vegetable oil is used to massage the nape or temples in case of sick headaches, see **description of the plant.**

- **Cassava or Yuca,** the powerful properties of the roots are anti-inflammatory, helping in the treatment of the general pain associated with sick headaches, see **description of the plant.**

- **Cloves,** against sick headaches, see **description of plant,** form of use **IV.**

- **Grape vine,** against sick headaches, the leaves in infusion are made with a dessert teaspoon of dried leaves per cup of water, for 10 minutes. Rest 10 minutes and take a spoonful every ¼ h., see **description of plant.**

- **Heath speedwell,** it is used to relieve **sick headaches of digestive origin,** see **description of the plant.**

- **Lemon verbena,** the infusion is used to treat sick headaches, see **description of the plant.**

- **Marjoram,** It is used to relieve sick headaches, see **description of plant.**

- **Rose hip / hep / haw,** the infusion helps in cases of sick headaches, see **description of the plant**, form of use **VII.**

- **Rosemary,** to treat sick headaches, **associated with Hepatobiliary Dyskinesia,** see **description of the plant,** form of use **VII (1).**

- **Sweetscented bedstraw,** l the infusion is a good sedative, hypnotic and **soothing of proven effects** against sick headaches, see **description of the plant,** form of use **VII.**

Sweeteners

The **glucose** is one of the main ingredients that brings **more energy** to our body. During **childhood,** consumption is very important as it plays a fundamental role in **the development of tissues.** The brain absorbs 20% of the glucose that is ingested, nourishes **the nervous system serving** for a perfect **physical and mental development.**

- **Its consumption** replenishes **glycogen deposits in muscles and liver.** It helps to **conciliate the sleep** thanks to its relaxing effect.
- **Its lack** increases the appetite and **can produce anxiety,** being necessary a daily dose of glucose either in pastry or fruit, but with **moderate consumption** to avoid other problems due to excess intake. There are sweeteners or syrups of different medicinal plants, choose the highest purity and **to avoid caries problems** it is advisable to **use only a few drops,** given its concentration in sugars is very high.
- **Low-glycemic** sweeteners **of less than 5%** are recommended **in children, also for diabetics, with diets or cholesterol problems,** preferably **0.2% Birch sugar** or **Stevia, without any sugar,** although with a slight licorice flavor.
- **The little** ones are often **reluctant to drink infusions, because of their taste,** but they can be masked with Mint, a drop of Vanilla or any sweetener pleasant to your palate (see possible contraindications or interactions).
- **Some adults do not support certain infusions,** i advise a similar solution, although **the best is unsweetened.**

Continue

Some sweeteners as an example

- **Acer,** excellent sweetener is the use of its honey (also known as Maple syrup) syrup extracted by the evaporation of the sap of the tree, contains a large amount of sugars simple and only 0.7% minerals. **Contraindicated for diabetics and persons intolerant to glucose,** see **description of plant.**

- **Apple,** there is a syrup of the apple ideal for the little ones, and with more food than refined sugar, it serves to vary the taste of any medicine or drink that should taken, see **description of the plant.**

- **Barley,** the molasses is obtained equal and with the same benefit as that of rice as sweetener. It is undoubtedly a good substitute for white sugar (completely devoid of nutrients), **especially for children,** see **description of the plant.**

- **Birch,** there is a hypoglycaemic sugar, with 0.2 gr. of sugar, very interesting for diabetics or diets, see **description of the plant.**

- **Blue agave,** With its it is possible a syrup that serves as a sweetener. There are different preparations being extremely sweet using only a few drops, being able to find one of low glycemic power, ideal for minors, persons with diets and diabetics, see **description of the plant.**

- **Coconut,** there is a sugar **the** coconut, see **description of the plant.**

- **Honey,** the honey can contain up to 150 different elements in its composition, very natural and delicious sweetener, but should be consumed in moderation, **only over 1 year,** see **description of the Honey.**

- **Larch tree,** in summer the leaves sweat a liquid that is used to sweeten, beneficial for persons with diabetes, see **description of the plant.**

- **Onion,** you can make onion molasses as a sweetener, it is obtained just like rice by decoction. It is a good substitute for white sugar (completely devoid of nutrients), **especially for children, see description of the plant.**

- **Polypodium fern,** the flavor of the root is sweet (contain sucrose), it can be used without any inconvenience as a sweetener. **It exists in powder form. Diabetics should consult the doctor or specialist,** see **description of the plant.**

- **Pryckli pear,** there is a sugar **the** pryckli pear, and an ideal sweetener molasses for diets containing 67% less calories than sugar. **Diabetics,** better to consult about different preparations, see **description of plant.**

- **Rice,** as a molasses is used as a sweetener, as it is a fermented product, its digestibility is greater, and it contains, just like whole cane sugar integral, a certain amount of vitamins and minerals from these cereals. Also, if they have been elaborated with temperatures below 70º C, they contain enzymatic properties so it is important to obtain them of good quality. Sweeten something less than sugar and they are quite soft on the palate. It is certainly a **good substitute for white sugar** (completely devoid of nutrients), especially for the child population. There is a **rice syrup** in the market, see **description of the plant.**

- **Stevia,** used as a sweetener is ideal against tooth decay and for diabetics as it does not contain sugar, being important in any diet due to its low calorie content, see **description of the plant.**

- **Strawberries,** there is a syrup of the strawberries ideal for the little ones, and with more food than refined sugar, it serves to vary the taste of any medicine or drink that should taken, see **description of the plant.**

- **Sugarcane,** the cane sugar integral, it is one of the sweeteners richest in vitamins and minerals. **Consider that even the excess of this sugar is detrimental to the dental health.** Varies the conditions **when used in juice,** it is important to consume the juice as soon as it is extracted, ...**Continue**

... it tends to oxidize in 15 minutes. The sugar is obtained by evaporating the cane juice by heating or lyophilization, **of all types of sugar is the healthiest, because contains some minerals and vitamins when the artisanal manufacturing process is respected.**

The real integral cane sugar is not brown, but it has a slightly toasted color and cakes easily on contact with moisture. **We will find it in stores specializing in biological products.** The one that is usually sold in hypermarkets is full of additives, it has nothing to do with the real thing. Neither the colour, nor the texture, nor its properties, nor the process of industrial production. There is also **cane molasses,** in specialized stores. **Contraindicated for diabetics and persons intolerant to the glucose,** see **description of the plant,** form of use **X.**

Form of use of plants with letters A - B

- Artichoke, eat the cooked artichokes and drink the resulting liquid, its properties are very depurative. Also raw or in juice by squeezing 1 teaspoon of its leaves finely cut, ½ bulb of Fennel, 4 green leaves of Dandelion, 4 stalks of Celery, ½ Zucchini, and dilute with a little mineral water, see **descriptions of the plants.**

- Ashwagandha or Indian ginseng, see **description of the plant.**
- **VII - The infusion** is done by boiling the root 15 minutes. Its flavor being very bitter to mask with other herbs or fruits in preparation. **It is found in powder** to add to beverages of sweet taste, for its bitter taste, although in this way it is difficult to quantify accurately the amount of the active ingredient that is ingested.
- **VII - In the form of capsules,** it is a way to improve its flavor and allows quantifying the amount of active ingredient that is ingested. Its effect is slow, take daily for a few weeks to observe the fullness of its beneficial effects.

- Ayahuasca, the cooking of its leaves, stem and seeds, taken in infusion, is the method for the remedies described, see **description of the plant.**

- **Barley,** see **description of the different plants.**
  - **VII - The decoction is made** with crushed barley (semolina preferably). Boil 40-50 gr. according to desired density, with semolina less quantity, for 10 minutes in 1 ½ liter of water with a cinnamon stick. Once it starts to boil, put on a low heat until 1 liter approx. Strain and use, **you can drink it as day water,** even **for baby bottles** mixed in juice or directly. The barley left in the colander can be used with yoghurts, in salads, baby porridge. **Also raw crushed barley** can be added to any stew and cook in turn **as a vitamin supplement.**

- **Bloodroot,** see **description of the plant.**
  - **VII - The infusion is made** by placing in a cup with boiling water some leaves of the plant. Drink hot, sweeten to taste.
  - **VII - Another infusion is made** with 20 gr. of the plant in 1 liter of water. Drink hot three times a day, sweeten to taste.

- **Blue passionflower**, see **description of the plant.**
  - **VII - Infusion,** 1 to 3 gr. per day (3 cups/day).
  - **VII - Fresh plant juice,** 2.5 ml (3 times daily).

- **Borage,** you should prepare **the infusion with a dessert spoonful** of the plant per cup of hot water, stand with the liquid covered 4 minutes, strain and drink warm, see **description of the plant.**

Form of use of plant with letter C

- **Cecropia,** see **description of the plant.**
  - **VII - The infusion it is made** pouring 20 gr. of leaves per liter of boiling water, boil 10 minutes more. Rest and strain, you can drink up to 3 cups. **It is recommended** to sweeten it to be very bitter.

- **Celery,** see **description of the plant.**
  - **In egg salad,** Celery leaves provide a substantial flavor to the mixture. Cut the upper part of the stems into fine pieces, with leaves and add to the boiled egg.   **Continue...**

...
- **Stuffed,** it works incredibly with any kind of bird. It can even be used to fill any bird in the oven.
- **Soups,** can be used in almost any soup. Put a little (or a lot) of Celery in the soup, always the same amount of Celery as Carrot
  - **Steamed,** it retains its flavor and nutrients by 99%, in the refrigerator, in an airtight container or by wrapping it in a plastic bag.

- Chestnut tree, see **description of the plant.**
- **VII (1) - The infusion ingested its made** with 60 gr. of leaves or crust per liter of water. Boil 15 minutes. Strain and drink 3 - 4 cups daily.

- Chicory, the infusion of its **leaves and roots,** in topical use, for its medicinal properties, it is used for bandages and poultices on wounds, contusions, acne, boils and cuts that need to heal, see **description of plant.**

- Cistus or Rockrose, make the **infusion with a little** of your labdanum in a cup of boiling water. Drink a maximum of 3 cups a day, **caution,** see **description of the plant.**

- Clary or Clary sage, see **description of the plants.**
- **VII (2). Nervousness,** mix 3.75 milliliters of Jojoba oil, 2 drops of Chamomile oil, 4 drops of Clary sage oil, 1 drop of Incense oil, 1 drop of Neroli oil and 3 drops of Orange oil. Mix and use as a fragrance or inhale from the bottle, as required.

- Cloves, see **description of the plant.**
- **IV - as a poultice and the preparation for massage** is done mixing with salt, water and Cloves, **against sick headaches.**

- Common poppy (seeds), see **description of the plant.**
- **VIII - In salads,** you can add to salads, a handful of seeds, after seasoned.
- **VIII - In soups and broths,** add a handful of soup or broth, it will add a nutty flavor
- **VIII - In yogurt,** a handful of seeds for breakfast or snack, to combat diarrhea.   **Continue on next page...**

...

- **VIII - Alone,** the simplest option if you do not want to add to any dish, take 2 tablespoons of seeds accompanied by a glass of water or natural fruit juice. **Chew well.**

- Cowslip primrose, see **description of the plant.**
- **VII - The infusion its made** with 60 gr. per liter of water. Boil, filter, rest for a few minutes. Drink 2 cups daily or gargle several times a day (no more than 4), **without sweetening.**

Form of use of plants with letters D - E - G

- Devil's Claw, the infusion of the ingested root should be taken at least 3 times a day if the ailment is persistent, see **description of the plant.**

- Elms, see **description of the plant.**
- **VII - The infusion its prepared** with 2 teaspoons of crust per liter of water. Boil, strain and drink. **Used** in topical use, **without sweetening.**

- Geranium or Cranesbills, see **description of the different plants.**
- **The infusion its made** with 4 gr. of root in 100 ml of water, it can be accompanied with infusions of Chamomile, Spearmint, Mint. For mouth and throat conditions, it is recommended every 4 hours, gargling **without sweetening.**

- Great mullein or Mullein, the infusion **is done with 3 or 4 gr. of the plant**, and drink 3 to 4 cups daily, at least for a week, see **description plant.**

Form of use of plants with letters H - J

- Hazel tree, see **description of the plant.**
- **IV - Prepare a decoction** of the roots with 30 gr. for 1 liter of water, boil 15 minutes, add ½ liter of 40º alcohol and mix to make compresses and poultices. **Continue...**

...

- **VII - The infusion it is made** boiling 25 gr. of leaves per liter of water, leave 10 minutes, **rest and drink (sweeten to taste), to use in topical use (without sweetening).**

- **Heliotropium,** the infusion **of the root** is done with a spoonful of dessert per cup, see **description of the plant.**

- **Herb Bennet,** see **description of the plant.**
  - **VII (1) - VII (1) - The infusion its made** boiling between 60 - 90 gr. of root in a liter of wáter, or something less weight if the root is dry. Drink 3 to 4 cups during the day.

- **Hogweed,** the infusion **to ingest is prepared** with a handful of fresh roots in a liter of water, take 2 to 4 cups a day. **Drinking maceration** it is done by pouring 3 tablespoons of the infusion into a glass of water and leave to macerate for 8 hours. Before ingesting, see **description of plant.**

- **Hops,** see **description of the plant.**
  - **The infusion of the flowers** is made with 25 gr. of flowers in a liter of water. Boil for 10 minutes. Strain and drink up to 3 times a day.
  - **The infusion of the grain,** boil 15 gr. in ½ liter of water. You should drink a cup on an empty stomach.

- **Horseradish,** see **description of the plant.**
  - **It is recommended from 3 to 5 gr. of the freshly grated root,** take three times daily, or in infusion of 2 to 3 ml. **The Nasturtium-horseradish is sold, follow the manufacturer's** or specialist's instructions.

- **Japanese buckwheat,** see **description of plants.**
  - **Form of consume VIII.**

One of the biggest **advantages of Buckwheat is that it is made very fast,** more than other cereals such as rice or millet. It takes about 15 minutes at low heat, without losing properties. **Ideal to use often.**

Continue on next page

...

- **Salads,** in summer, a good way to take cereals and legumes. **The Buckwheat combines** well with any raw vegetable in salad of Broccoli, Tomato, Lettuce, Zucchini, etc.).
- **Stew/Potaje,** in winter, instead, we can take **Buckwheat** in the form of stew and 20 minutes before removing from the fire, **Potatoes and Buckwheat.** With Lentils, (lentils take 5 minutes to soften).
- **Purees and creams,** both in winter (puree) and in summer (cold cream), you can cook some legumes, some vegetables and Buckwheat. For example, make a rich purée with Azúkis beans, Buckwheat and Cabbage.

Form of use of plants with letters L -M - N

- **Large-leaved linden,** the **infusion is made** by boiling a cup of water with a handful of flowers from the tree or about 6 leaves in its absence. Rest 5 minutes, strain and drink. In inhalations, rinses or gargles, **without sweetening,** see **description of the plant.**

- **Motherwort,** see **description of the plant.**
- The flowering tops, preferably fresh, are used. The dried leaves blacken and lose their medicinal efficacy. Boil, stand 10 minutes, strain and drink tempered, **without sweetening.**
- **VII - Infusion:** as a tonic it is made with 30 to 50 gr. of flowering tops in a liter of boiling water. Strain and take 3 cups a day. It can also be used in topical use
- **VII - Tisane:** against palpitations or tachycardia. 150 gr. of leaves, 50 gr. of Valerian root and 100 gr. of Rosemary leaves. Boil in a liter of water for 5 minutes. Filter and drink several days, a very hot cup at night before bedtime
- **VII - As a tranquilizer:** two large spoonfuls of Motherwort in 250 gr. of boiling water. Stand, strain and drink.

- **Myrtle,** see **description of the plant.**
  - **VII - The infusion its made** with a teaspoon of leaves per-cup of water. Also with 15 gr. of leaves per liter of water.

- **Narrow-leaf strap fern,** see **description of the plant**
  - **VII - As day water** add a portion of root previously washed, chopped and crushed in a liter of water. Boil until the liquid is reduced by half, drink, sweetening to taste.
  - **VII - Preparation of infusions:** use 20 gr. of the rhizome or root in half a liter of boiling water and drink, sweetening to taste.

Form of use of plants with letters O - P

- **Oregano,** see **description of the plant.**
  - **VII - The infusion its made** with one tablespoon of dessert per-cup. Boil for 10 minutes, strain and drink 3 times a day, before or after meals.

- **Perforate St John's-wort or Hyperucum,** see **descriptions plants.**
  - **VII (1) - Infusion,** is made by boiling parts of the plant for 3 minutes. Rest 5 minutes, strain and drink 2 to 3 cups daily, sweeten to taste.
- **Against depression,** there are different types of pathologies added, there are different ways to combat them apart from No. 1 and are:
  - **VII (2) - To enhance the No. 1, if necessary,** put hypericum, water lily, oregano and sage. In equal parts, the measurement is 2 teaspoons of the mixture per cup in infusion. Rest for 5 minutes. Strain and drink three cups a day, fasting or between meals.
  - **VII (3) - For depression accompanied by insomnia,** plants: Briar root/Heather, Horehound, Linden Tree and Perforate St John's-wort/ Hypericum and Valerian root, in equal parts. Boil the mixture, per cup, for 2 minutes over low heat and clogged. Rest for 5 minutes, strain and drink a cup after dinner

Continue on next page

...

- **VII (4) - For depression and shyness,** plants: Illyrian king plant/Gentian/Gentius plant, Perforate St John's-wort/Hypericum, Rosemary and Summer savory in equal parts. Boil a teaspoon of the mixture per cup in infusion, rest a few minutes. Strain and drink one cup at breakfast and another after lunch.

- **Pollen,** see **description of Pollen.**
- How to **measure the doses** of dry pollen to ingest:
  - 1 teaspoon of coffee rasa = 5 gr.
  - 1 teaspoon of coffee filled = 8 gr.
  - 1 spoonful of dessert rasa = 10 gr.
  - 1 heaping dessert spoonful = 15 gr.
  - 1 tablespoon rasa soup = 15 gr.
  - 1 tablespoon of heaped soup = 25 gr

- It is recommended to take pollen for 20 days, and rest 10 days, continue, for the recovery of health and vigor.
  - **VIII (1) - Adults,** 4 teaspoons of coffee filled (32 gr). For maintenance 2 teaspoons of dessert rasas (20 gr.
  - **VIII (2) - Children between 3 and 5 years,** a little less than one heaped dessert spoonful (12 gr.)
  - **VIII (3) - Children between 6 and 12 years,** a little more than a teaspoon of plain soup (16 gr.)
  - **VIII (4) - Children over 12 years,** 2 tablespoons of dessert rasas (20 gr.)

- **Pomegranate,** see **description of the plants and of the Honey.**
  - **VIII - Preferably consumed on an empty stomach,** to extract the seeds simply to cut it in half and hit the part of the shell with a spoon. It can also be cut in four quarters to go taking off the seeds more easily.
  VIII - You can make juice with its seeds or use the commercialized one, better to sweeten with Stevia or Honey. The juice leaves a slightly harsh feeling on the tongue, for the tannins, of astringent property. It can be mixed with Apple, Orange, Carrot, Ginger. **Persons with constipation should not abuse pomegranate juice.**

- **Primrose,** the infusion **is prepared with** a spoonful of root dessert preferably, or with fresh or dried flowers per cup of water. Boil, stand 5 minutes, drink two or three cups daily, see **description of the plant.**

- **Psoralea or Otholobium,** see **description of the plant.**
  - **VII - The infusion its prepared** with 30 gr. of leaves per ½ litre of water, boil for 30 minutes. Rest for a few minutes and use. **In washes,** rinses or gargles, **without sweetening.**

Form of use of plants with letters R - S

- **Rose hip / hep / haw,** The base **infusion is done with** a spoonful of crust, fresh or dry, for different ailments, see **description of the plant.**

- **Rosemary,** see **descriptions of the plants.**
  - **VII (1) - Infusion to ingest,** put a teaspoon (of dessert) of leaves and flowers in a cup with boiling water. Boil 10 minutes, drink 3 cups a day, before or after meals.
  - **VII (2) - Decoction in topical use,** with 30-40 gr./l, boil 10 minutes. Apply in the form of baths, washes or compresses embedded.
  - **VII (3) - Essential oil,** dilute between 2 or 5%, in alcoholic or oily solution, before using.
- **More complex and potent form of the infusion to ingest. It is recommended to store in separate containers and properly labeled, see descriptions.**
  - **In the morning,** drink an infusion of Rosemary, Horsetail and Boldo. The herbs are mixed in equal parts and stored in an airtight container and in a place without light. When boiling the water, pour a teaspoon filled with the above mixture, let stand for 5 minutes and drink.
  - **After meals,** it is recommended to drink an infusion of Horsetail, Dandelion, Anise seeds and Chamomile flowers. These herbs should be mixed and stored as indicated, in a sealed container and protected from light, prepared in the same way as the previous récipe.

Continue on next page

...

- **At night,** an infusion of Horsetail, Tila/ Large-leaved lime, Mistletoe, Hawthorn and Chamomile flowers is recommended, follow the same indications above.

- **Senecio oreophyton,** the infusion **is made** by boiling 20 gr. In 1 litre of water for 10 minutes, straining and drinking 3 cups a day. **It is powered** by honey **(over 1 year),** or sweetened to taste, see   see **description of the plant and Honey.**

- **Sweetscented bedstraw,** used as **a soother,** of proven effects, in ¼ liter of boiling water, pour 1 teaspoon of dessert full of dried grass, rest 5 minutes. Strain and sweeten with honey **(over 1 year),** drink immediately before going to bed, see **description of the plant and Honey.**

Form of use of plants with letters V-W-Y

- **Vervain,** see **description of the plant.**
  - **VII (1) - The ingested infusion** is made in a cup of mineral water. When breaking to boil add 2 dessert spoons of leaves, dry. Rest 10 minutes, strain and drink warm 2 or 3 times a day, sweeten to taste.
  - **VII (2) - In topical use,** place 3 tablespoons of dried leaves in a cup of mineral water. When it breaks to boil let simmer 15 minutes. Strain, cool **and unsweetened** moisten the dressing or compress to place on the forehead for 5 minutes, repeat until discomfort is passed.
  - **VII (3) - Another form of topical use,** place a handful of fresh leaves in a glass of vinegar, simmer until the vinegar evaporates. Wrap the leaves, warm in gauze or compress and apply on the painful area.

- **Wood violet,** see **description of the plant.**
  - **VII - The infusion** should be made with half a teaspoon of dried flower dessert, in a cup of boiling water, rest a few minutes, strain and drink.
  - **VII - The decoction** is done with 50 gr. of root per liter of water. It is recommended to drink several cups a day.

- Yarrow, the infusion **should be taken** a cup 3 times a day in cases of anxiety, depression, stress or nerves, see **description of the plant.**

Descriptions of plants letter A

- Acer
- Ajuga iva
- Allspice, see Jamaica pepper
- Aloe vera
- Amla, see Indian gooseberry
- Apple
- Aromita, see Vachellia aroma
- Artichoke
- Asafoetida
- Ashwagandha
- Ayahuasca
- Azuki red beans

Acer, (Arce, en español)

Hacer saccharum", tree originating to Asia and abundant North America where 160 species, are also cultivated as ornamental trees, for the exploitation of its wood in the construction and for the elaboration of maple syrup (also called Maple honey), the largest production place of this syrup is Quebec (Canada). The leaf is the symbol of Canada, appearing on its flag. **Contraindicated for diabetics** (due to its high concentration of sugars) **and persons intolerant to glucose.**

Ajuga iva, (Ajuga iva, en español)

Ajuga iva", originating from southern Europe in the Mediterranean area. The ingested infusion is made by boiling about 15 gr. for each liter of water for 15 minutes, rest and strain, take a cup on an empty stomach. **To reinforce its effects** you can have another cup in the afternoon. **Contraindicated in persons suffering from gastritis or gastroduodenal ulcer.**

Aloe vera, (Aloe vera, en español)

Aloe arborescens", is one of the pharmaceutical applications, oldest registered, is found in a Sumerian clay tablet, there are drawings of the plant on the walls of Egyptian temples. Originating from North Africa, of fleshy leaves used for the treatment of ...**Continue on nex page**

... many health problems, it is recommended especially for skin problems in poultice or directly its inner gel. Two compounds, gel and juice are obtained from the leaves. **Special care with your gel, if ingested.** There are juice preparations. **Contraindicated the juices in pregnant women (abortive), or lactation, under 12 years, patients with irritable bowel, colitis, Crohn's disease, hemorrhoids, diabetics.**

- Apple, (Manzana, en español)

"Malus domestica", plant domesticated more than 15 thousand years ago, of Caucasian origin on the banks of the Caspian Sea, introduced in Europe by the Romans. It is one of the most complete and nutritious fruits. Studies are being conducted on seeds as anticarcinogenic, with surprising results and beneficial against all types of cancers. **The contraindications of apples are mainly due to their bad consumption:** when they are very green, without chewing well, badly washed. **Acid apples are harmful for:** persons suffering from constipation, urethral stricture and severe stomach conditions by excess ingestion (worse if they are not mature enough). **Sour apples are contraindicated for persons with a stomach ulcer.**

- Artichoke, (Alcachofa, en español)

It is called the fruit of the plant "Cynara scolymus", originally from the western Mediterranean. It is one of the vegetable sources richest in calcium, iron, magnesium and potassium. It also contains fiber and Cinarina. It can be found in capsules and extracts. It can cause: flatulence and allergies. **Consult the doctor:** those prone to gallstones. **Consume with moderation** the hypertensive. **Contraindicated in pregnancy or lactation women.**

- Asafoetida, (Asafétida, en español)

"Ferula assafoetida", also know a Devil's dung, it grows mainly in Afghanistan and Northern Iran, its resin is exported to India, there called Hing. It is marketed mainly in yellowish powder consisting of the mixture of ground resin with rice or wheat. **Very difficult to find, only in Indian shops.** Plant with nauseating odor in raw, cooked softens and produces a flavor similar to onion and garlic, it is used ...**Continue**

... as a condiment in the form of a spice. **There are no known contraindications,** it is **recommended to consult** with the doctor or specialist.

- Ashwagandha, (Ashwagandha, en español)

"Whitania somnifera", also know as Indian ginseng, originally from the mountains of the Himalayas, it is used to increase the immune system that protects us against infections and diseases. Taken **in the morning** increases your energy levels, **at night** helps you sleep better. **Contraindicated in pregnancy, and persons immunosuppressants.**

- Ayahuasca, (Ayahuasca, en español)

"Banisteriopsis caapi", considered in the Amazon as the spirit of Nature. According to studies carried out the use of Ayahuasca has an approximate age of 5,000 years. **Use under medical prescription.** The decoction of its leaves, stem and seeds and in infusion is used. **Caution is advised in its use, may cause nausea, paleness/pallor, pupillary dilation, salivation, profuse sweating, and in some cases fatal intoxication.**

- Azuki red beans, (Azúkis, en español)

"Vigna angularis, var. nipponensis", originating from China, from there he went to Japan where it has become one of its main crops. It is consumed equal to any legume, soaking it 8 hours before cooking. Gluten-free, ideal food for any diet. With a not very high amount of fat, **it is advisable consume in moderate amounts in persons with a diet of weight loss, high uric acid, hyperthyroidism, gout and prone to flatulence.**

Descriptions of plants letter B

- Baikal skullcap
- Banana
- Barley
- Beet
- Bergamot orange
- Birch
- Bitter kola
- Bitter lettuce
- Bitter orange
- Bitter wood
- Black henbane
- Black sesame
- Blackcurrant
- Bloodroot

- Blue agave
- Blue passionflower, see Passionflower
- Blueweed, see Viper's bugloss
- Boldo
- Borage
- Brazil nut
- Briar root
- Broad-leaved paperbark, see, Niaouli
- Bruisewort, see Common Daisy
- Bull bay, see Southern magnolia
- Butterbur

- Baikal skullcap, (Escutelaria china, en español)

"Scutellaria baicalensis", one of the 50 most used plants in traditional Chinese medicine, known as Huan qin. Native to Central Asia and North America. It is used in remedies and preparations against fever the infusion of the aerial part of the plant. There are also tinctures and capsules. **It can cause side effects such as:** drowsiness, confusion and lightheadedness. **Contraindicated the extract during pregnancy and lactation.**

- Banana, (Plátano, en español)

"Musa paradisiaca", originating from India, highly nutritious and of the most caloric fruits that exist after the avocado, 100 gr. of banana contribute approximately 90 calories. Very rich in carbohydrates being one of the best ways to nourish our body with vegetable energy, very indicated in the diets of children for their properties and benefits. **In excess** can be indigestible. Diabetics should consume sparingly. **Persons with kidney or liver diseases,** it is **recommended to consult** with the doctor or specialist.

- Barley, (Cebada, en español)

"Hordeum vulgare", originating from the Middle East, food-medicine that can be consumed in diverses forms, such as semolina, cooked in any stew, salad, milk or as day water. **Contraindicated in persons with hypersensitivity to barley flour, allergic to beer, celiac and hypertensive (with assiduity).**

- Beet, (Remolacha, en español)
"Beta vulgaris", originating from Mediterranean, very humble vegetable, but with surprising properties. **Consume with moderation persons with:** stomach acidity, gastritis, hypotension, gout, arthritis or kidney problems. **Contraindicated in pregnancy women and diabetics.**

- Bergamot orange, (Bergamota, en español)
"Citrus bergamia", originally from Persia as a result of the graft between the Key lime and the Bitter Orange. The fruit and the infusions its used to healing remedies The best medicinal or cosmetic properties are achieved through its essential oil, like balm, **after its application, do not expose yourself to the sun. Do not consume the juice or fruit in combination with drugs.**

- Birch, (Abedul, en español)
"Betula pendula", also know as Silver birch, of origin Eurasian, almost silvery white crust. **It is used almost entirely:** leaves, flowers, sap, buds and crust of young branches. **There is essential oil, not ingest (toxic and deadly). Only for topical use and always diluted as directed by the specialist.** It is used for the infusion of tree buds and the crust. **Contraindicated during pregnancy or lactation, persons with hydrops of cardiac or renal origin, allergic and hypertensive,** (only under prescription and medical control).

- Bitter kola, (Nuez de Cola, en español)
"Garcinia kola", originally from Africa, similar to the oriental, its fruit is the Cola Nut (bitter Kola), fruit with diverse properties and uses. It can be consumed in infusions, alone, with honey, chewed directly, liquefied as a soft drink or powdered. **Its side effects could be:** nervousness, insomnia, headaches. **A lot of caution if you have:** tachycardia, hypertension, gastric ulcers, insomnia or difficulty falling asleep. **Contraindicated in pregnant women, and children under 12 years of age.**

- Bitter lettuce, (Lechuga virosa, en español)
"Lactuca virosa L", originating from Central Asia, Egyptian papyri date their use for various ailments towards 1,600 BC of yellow flowers and unpleasant smell. **It is used in substitution of opium, ...Continue on next page**

...but without harmful side effects. At present it is mainly used as a calming, in syrup and associated with Hops. **Do not exceed the indicated doses, use only under medical supervision.** You can use the common lettuce already spiked. **The juice or latex is toxic.**

- Bitter orange, (Naranjo amargo, en español)

"Citrus aurantium", also know as Seville orange, It is the most fragrant species of the 15 that comprises the genus Citrus. Its flowers are used in cosmetics (orange blossom water), The crust for the elaboration of the "Curaçao liqueur", the fruit for the manufacture of jams and the leaves for the elaboration of infusions. **It can produce cardiovascular adverse effects, in heart rate, in blood pressure,** boosted by caffeine, so it is not advisable to use it together. Juice can cause migraines in persons who are sensitive to it. The fruits are used, ingested or externally, the leaves, flowers in infusion, also their essential oil, called Neroli (it is treated later). **Administer the juice with great caution in:** pregnant and under 2 years yeras, never exceed the indicated quantities. **Contraindicated in persons with: severe hypertension, diabetes mellitus, glaucoma and prostatic hypertrophy, in treatment with MAOI** (antidepressant inhibitors of the enzyme Mono Amino Oxidase). **Simultaneous with medicines containing:** Ciclosporin.

- Bitter wood, (Quassia, en español)

"Quassia Amara" or "Picrama excelsa", originating from Tropical America and one of the most bitter plants that exist. Very used for cosmetic and medicinal purposes. Stands out for being a natural insecticide very efficient to not contain toxic substances, does not affect pets or children and repels all kinds of insects being economic and ecological. **The crust in infusion only under specialist control. Quassia vinegar is also used. Contraindicated during the menstrual period (may cause colics, pain and increased uterine tone) and pregnant women (abortive).**

- Black henbane, (Beleño negro, en español)

"Hyoscyamus niger", **poisonous plant,** native to Eurasia, grows at the feet of walls, areas of rubble and dunghills. Some of its alkaloids are of excellent properties on the central nervous system. **Use only the leaves, with extreme caution. Under medical prescription.**

- Black sesame, (Sésamo, en español)

"Sesamum indicum", originating from India and Africa, from where it arrived in America transported by the slaves. It can be consumed directly in salads, sweets, rice, grilled or sautéed vegetables. **Use only under medical prescription:** persons with liver or kidney disease. **Contraindicated the esential oil in pregnancy women.**

- Blackcurrant, (Grosellero negro, en español)

"Ribes nigrum", originating from central and eastern Europe. With it are madejams, syrups or juices. The medicinal properties for healing purposes are the leaves and buds in infusions, also the ingested fruits or in juices, and even the oil obtained from the seeds. **Under prescription and medical control as a diuretic and against uric acid, in the presence of hypertension, heart disease or moderate or severe renal failure.**

- Bloodroot, (Sanguinaria del Canadá, en español)

"Sanguinaria canadensis", originating from USA and Canada, of white or pink flowers. **For curative purposes, the leaves are used in infusion. There are dental products with bloodroot. Before using to consult** with the doctor or specialist, It has toxic alkaloids like Opium and can irritate the mucous membrane. **Contraindicated in pregnancy or lactation women.**

- Blue agave, (Agave tequilana, en español)

"Agave tequilana", also know as Tequila agave, originating from Mesoamerica, with it Tequila is made, but it is mainly used for its medicinal properties for both topical and internal use by infusions of the leaves, if you want to sweeten, see the sweeteners. With this plant is also used made a syrup that serves as a sweetener. If there are **allergic reactions** such as **difficulty breathing, rash, swelling of the lips or tongue, seek urgent medical attention. It can produce:** diarrhea and upset stomach. **Contraindicated during pregnancy or lactation women.**

- **Boldo,** (Boldo, en español)

"Peumus boldus", tree native to Chile and the only species of this genus. Never use more than 4 weeks, with 2 months interval, between each one. **Contraindicated in pregnant women, infants, children under 12 years of age and persons with vesicular, hepatic or renal disease obstructions.**

- **Borage,** (Borraja, en español)

"Borago officinalis", originally from North Africa and the Middle East. With the seeds an oil is elaborated for different therapeutic remedies. **Contraindicated for pregnant, children under 6 years and liver.**

- **Briar root or Heater,** (Brezo, en español)

"Erica arbórea", originally from the Mediterranean, with medicinal properties for internal and external use, the flowers are used to make infusions to drink or in topical use. **Excessively it may cause gastric discomfort so the doctor should be consulted on the dose and time of treatment to be followed. Do not consume for children under 6 years, persons with gastritis, gastroduodenal ulcer or with ethyl problems.**

- **Brazil nut,** (Nuez de Brasil, en español)

"Bertholletia excelsa", fruit of a tree that grows in Bolivia, Brazil, southeastern Colombia. The shells contain high amounts of aflatoxins, a natural toxic substance **that can cause liver cancer.** The fruit has a high Selenium content of possible toxicity, its excess can cause the nails and hair to become fragile and fall. **The allergic to nuts should be extremely careful with this,** being the most serious of allergies, leading to consequences that can endanger life. **Limit its use with people with high cholesterol or triglycerides. Contraindicated children under 3 years.**

- **Butterbur,** (Sombrerera, en español)

"Petasites hybridus", native to Europe and North Asia, it grows in the vicinity of forests, in humid areas. It is used for therapeutic remedies the root. There are tinctures for topical use or ingestion. **Always with medical control to prescribe the right dosage.** Also the dry infusion plant that is prepared by boiling ¼ liter of water, pouring 2 teaspoons of coffee with the herb. Rest a few minutes, filter and drink, you can take 1 or 2 cups a day. **Excessive doses or prolonged use may ...Continue on next page**

... **cause serious problems in:** liver, gastrointestinal mucosa, loss of appetite, ascites, abdominal pain. **Contraindicated in pregnant women, infants, children under 12 years and hypotensive persons.**

Descriptions of plants letter C

- Cacao
- Calamintha
- Calamus
- Camomile, see Chamomile
- Camphor tree
- Cananga tree, see Ylang Ylang
- Caraway, see Meridian fennel
- Carolina Jasmine, see Yellow jessamine
- Cassava
- Catnip
- Cecropia
- Cedar oil
- Celery
- Chachacoma
- Chameleon vine, see Orange flame vine
- Chamomile
- Chaste tree, see Vitex
- Cherimoya
- Cherry
- Chestnut tree
- Chickpea
- Chicory
- Chili pepper
- Chinese ginseng, see Ginseng
- Chinese wolfberry
- Chives
- Cinnamon with honey
- Cissampelos pareira
- Cistus
- Clary sage or Clary
- Cloves
- Cocoa, see Cacao
- Coconut tree/Coconut
- Coffe
- Common daisy
- Common hawthorn
- Common lady's mantle
- Common poppy
- Common primrose, see English primrose

- Common soapwort
- Copalchi
- Corn mint, see Wild mint
- Corydalis cava
- Cowslip primrose
- Cranesbills, see Geranium
- Cucumber
- Cumin

- Cacao or Cocoa, (Cacao, en español)

"Theobroma cacao", of Mexican origin, in the Mayan culture was used as currency of change. **Powerful food with incredible properties and benefits for our physical health, emotions and mental health.** Stimulates, comforts and revives the organism. One of the best known foods that exist, especially because you get one of the most consumed desserts par excellence: **chocolate. Contraindicated consumption in persons with constipation, hemorrhoids, hypertensive or nervous states (to contain traces of caffeine).**

- Calamintha, (Calamento, en español)

"Calamintha sylvatica", native to North africa, it is possible to find in low-fat forests of Asia and Europe. Its essential oil is used orally and in topical use. **Only use 1 drop. Do not use in the long term. Contraindicated in pregnant or lactating women.**

- Calamus, (Cálamo aromático, en español)

"Acorus calamus", also know as Sweet flag, it grows in the northern hemisphere on the banks of rivers and marshes. The medicinal use is very diverse for a long time, It gives off a pleasant smell, for the medicinal remedies the rhizome and the stems are used. **Discontinuous treatment is recommended,** one of its components **is suspected of producing cancer and toxic to the central nervous system. Contraindicated the essential oil in pregnancy or** lactation women **and children under 2 years.**

- Camphor tree, (Alcanforero, en español)

"Cinnamomum camphora", formerly from this tree was extracted camphor, is native Borneo, the oil **in excessive doses can be toxic and cause serious disorders for the organism. Limiting its use for joint pain and rheumatism,** diluting a few drops of camphor oil with olive oil or soap, helps to lessenand and reduce inflammation of the pain. ...**Continue**

... Contraindicated in pregnancy or lactation women, children under 12 years and in persons with Parkinson's, or epilepsy.

- Cassava or Yuca, (Mandioca o Yuca, en español)

"Manihot esculenta", also know as Manioc, Native from America, from southern Mesoamerica to the Caribbean. For therapeutic uses the herb, root and crust are used in extracts. **The extracts may cause minor side effects in some persons, such as:** upset stomach, nausea and oral irritation. An effective dose of extract would be between 2 to 4 gr. per day. **The tea prepared with the extract can be taken up to three times a day. Overdose or long-term use of the herb may cause diarrhea.**

- Catnip, (Gatera, en español)

"Nepeta cataria", originating from Europe, the Romans already used it for curative purposes, **also against smallpox and scarlet fever.** Its name is due to its effects on the behavior of cats, both in domestic animals and in larger ones (even in big cats). It is consumed mainly in the form of tea, preparing the infusion with a teaspoon of the plant for each cup of water, boil, let stand 3 minutes, strain and drink. It can also be used in juice, tincture, poultice, chew and even smoked. **Contraindicated in pregnant women.**

- Cecropia, (Ambay, en español)

"Cecropia adenopus", tree originating in south America in its jungle areas. Its leaves and crust are used in infusion, **in topical use without sweetening.** Used for curative purposes by the aborigines from Mexico to the northeast region of Argentina, it continues to be a remedy of habitual use in the popular medicine of center and south of America. **Contraindicated in pregnancy or lactation women.**

- Cedar oil, (Aceite de Cedro, en español)

"Cedrus Atlántica", its oil is used in gargles or phytotherapy after breakfast and at bedtime. **Do not use more than 2 weeks in a row.** Use half a cup of water with a spoonful of sea salt and a drop of this oil in gargles or washes. **Contraindicated in pregnant women (abortive), or lactation, chlidren under 12 years. Patients with gastritis, gastroduodenal ulcers, irritable bowel, ulcerative colitis, Crohn's disease, ...Continue on next page**

... liver patients, epileptics, Parkinson's or other neurological diseases. Or inhalations in children under 6 years of age, persons with respiratory allergies or known hypersensitivity to this or other essential oils.

- Celery, (Apio, en español)

"Apium graveolens", originally from the Mediterranean basin, a well-known and easy to reproduce plant, it can be ingested raw, cooked or in juice. **Contraindicated in pregnant women (abortive),** see forms consume **VIII.**

- Chachacoma, (Chachacoma, en español)

"Senecio oreophyton", originating from argentinean-chilean mountain range and used since time immemorial by the aborigines of the area. There are several types, as a medicinal herb two have been recognized, **a white call,** whose healing properties and appearances are identical, differing only by the white color taken by the leaves and branches one of them. The usual form is the infusion, there are also syrups, and tinctures. **There are no known contraindications,** it is **recommended to consult** with the doctor or specialist.

- Chamomile or Camomile, (Manzanilla, en español)

"Chamaemelum nobile", originating from Europe, annual aromatic herb of the family of the compounds, can reach up to 60 cm. high. It grows on cultivated land, on sandy soil and barrens. The usual use is infusion ingested or in topical use. There is also essential oil, which should **not be mixed with alcohol. Contraindicated the essential oil in pregnant women (abortive), under 6 years.**

- Cherimoya, (Chirimoya, en español)

"Annona cherimola", originating from the Andean zone bordering Ecuador and Peru. Spain is the world's leading producer of cherimoya with 80% of the total. It does not need any treatment, it is eaten as is. **It is not recommended for dessert after a copious meal.** When consuming for the first time persons with problems of constipation may appear intestinal alteration, but it is really helping to correct your problem. Fruit of easy digestion very advisable in weak persons, ...**Continue**

... convalescents, elderly, in dyspepsia and especially in children and pregnant women. Some products extracted from the seeds from cherimoya They have been applied successfully in investigations for the treatment of lice, dysentery, headaches, gout and stones. **Potassium source, persons with kidney failure should be careful. Consume with moderation diabetics**.

- Cherry, (Cereza, en español)

Fruit of the Cherry tree, considered the super fruit, with multiple properties and health benefits. No limit in taking all the fruit you want. **There are no known contraindications,** it is **recommended to consult** with the doctor or specialist.

- Chestnut fruit, (Castaña, en español)

It is the fruit of the chestnut tree, cooked is delicious, it is made the exquisite Marron glacé (original Asturian form, but commercialized with that name by the French). We know it in the cold months, and the best way to consume is roasted. **Consume with moderation pregnant women. Contraindicated in diabetics.**

- Chestnut tree, (Castaño, en español)

"Castanea sativa", "Castanea sativa", tree originating from southern Europe and Asia Minor. It is used for medicinal remedies the bark, wood, leaves and buds. **There are no known contraindications,** it is **recommended to consult** with the doctor or specialist.

- Chickpea, (Garbanzo, en español)

"Cicer arietinum", its origin is believed in the eastern Mediterranean zone, legume rich in slowabsorbing carbohydrates, so it provides energy, but with very controlled blood sugar levels. **Control its use in:** slimming diets, with high uric acid levels, hyperthyroidism, goiter or thyroid nodules. **Persons who suffer from flatulence or can not consume a lot of insoluble fiber is better to eat eliminating the skin once cooked.**

- Chicory, (Achicoria, en español)

"Cichorium intybus", of origin Europe in a wild way, with numerous medical properties. Known for being an excellent substitute for coffee. Two cups of chicory infusion per day or a single cup before dinner are recommended. **Contraindicated in persons with low blood pressure, or if they have gallstones.**

- Chili pepper, (Guindilla, en español)

"Capsicum frutescens", pepper subgroup "Capsicum annuum", originally from Mexico and South America, discovered by Columbus and popularized throughout the world, they have had different **uses of popular tradition. The abuse can produce: diarrhea, gastritis, and damage to the liver and kidneys. Consume with moderation persons with stomach ulcers or heartburn, hepatitis, hemorrhoids and pregnant women.**

- Chinese wolfberry, (Goji, en español)

"Lycium barbarum", native of the Himalayas, its berries are one of the best foods to fight aging, and more dense in nutrients on the planet earth for its wide range of phytonutrients, antioxidants, vitamins, in its various forms. **It can also** be taken in juices. **Very careful when buying, that does not carry the preservative E-220, causes:** diarrhea, nausea and headaches. **Do not take with allergy to pollen.** Studies that warn of the **possible interaction** of the anticoagulant **Warfarin** as well as **possible side effects with the medicament Sintrom.** Consume in the morning because of its tendency to cause **insomnia.**

- Chives, (Cebollino, en español)

"Allium schoenoprasum", originating from the extreme north of the lands that today are part of Canada and Siberia. It can be used in soups, salads, sauces, tortillas, creams and various meals. For health benefits should be consumed on a daily basis, **not in large quantities.** Very easy to cultivate and in little space, you can have at home a pot of chives for fresh daily consumption. **There are no known contraindications,** it is **recommended to consult** with the doctor or specialist.

- Cinnamon / Cinnamon tree, (Canela / Canelo, en español)

"Cinnamomum verum" or "Drimys winteri", from Patagonia in Chile and Argentina. Evergreen tree, and sacred to the Mapuche people. The cinnamon is extracted from its crust to sprinkle, the infusion is made by adding hot water in a cup with bark, rest 5 minutes and drink hot. Giving flavor is not the only function, it has a lot of medicinal properties. **Contraindicated in pregnancy or lactation women.**

- Cinnamon with honey, (Canela con miel, en español)

Cinnamon and honey are two nutritious foods, **(use honey from 1 year).** It is prepared by mixing the honey and cinnamon until it is quite thick. Store the preparation in a hermetically sealed glass jar. Keep in a cool place, it keeps well for quite some time without the need for any preservative for the properties of both. A tablespoon with warm water daily cinnamon and honey has many properties for health and also with a delicious flavor. It can be mixed with other drinks.

- Cissampelos pareira, (Pareira brava, en español)

"Cissampelos Pareira" originating from Central and South America, wild plant that grows in all the warm and temperate regions of the world. Used in traditional Chinese and Ayurveda medicine since ancient times, as well as in Mexican indigenous medicine and other places in the world. All parts of the plant have healing properties. **Dosage under medical prescription** used in powder or capsules. **The excess, due to its diuretic effect, can produce various disorders.**

- Cistus or Rockrose, (Jara, en español)

"Cistus", native to the Mediterranean undergrowth. **Toxic plant** whose handling should be left in the hands of specialized personnel and **not in a homemade form.** For medicinal purposes the leaves and the oleoresin, called Labdanum, are extracted from the flowering tops the essence of cistus/rockrose, **this essence is very toxic, better to use the preparations.** It is rich in a substance called Ladaniol, a doughy mass that softens easily due to the heat. **Do not consume in the case of autoimmune diseases. In large quantities it can become toxic to the liver and nervous system.**

- Clary sage or Clary, (Salvia romana, en español)

"Salvia sclarea", originating from the Mediterranean basin to central Asia. **Do not drink alcohol using essential oil,** exaggerate alcoholic effects, drunkenness, later discomfort or cause drowsiness. **Contraindicated oil in pregnant women by stimulating menstrual flow.**

- Cloves, (Clavo, en español)

"Syzygium aromaticum", originally from Indonesia, it has been **used as a natural remedy for more than 2,000 years**, from the Egyptians to the Chinese, to the Greeks and Arabs. As benefits of the tree are mainly flower buttons, dried, used to relieve pain, have analgesic properties and to reduce inflammation. There is **essential oil** that must be used with extreme caution, **it can be poisonous.** Use in small quantities to be extremely strong, for its disinfectant and antiseptic effects. **Do not stay on the skin for a long time,** it can produce burns and irritations. **Contraindicated in pregnancy, or lactation women, children under 6 years. Persons suffering from gastritis, irritable bowel, respiratory allergies, Parkinson's.**

- Coconut tree/Coconut, (Cocotero/Coco, en español)

"Cocos nucifera", tree of unknown origin, Asian or Caribbean, does not tolerate the cold. Its fruit, the coconut, is the largest seed that exists of benefits and health properties consumed occasionally and naturally, unpackaged. Coconut oil contains high levels of lauric acid, and can be used for cooking. **Contraindicated in persons with some cardiovascular disease (contains many saturated fatty acids), high cholesterol or with weight control diet.**

- Coffe, (Café o Cafeto, en español)

"Coffea", native of Africa and Asia, although the origin is attributed in Abyssinia - Ethiopia, drink often controversial, but generally harmless for health even if it is decaffeinated. The results of a recent study, shows that **it is beneficial to drink between 3 and 5 cups.** If you want to sweeten, see the sweeteners. **High dose can produce:** headache, nausea, insomnia (in many cases) and dependence (in some cases). **Contraindicated in pregnancy, or lactation women, children under 12 years, liver patients, or with heart disease, ulcers, gastritis.**

- Common Daisy, (Margarita, en español)

"Bellis perennis", also know as Daisy or Bruisewort, originating from western, central and northern Europe. Its flowers and leaves are used for the treatment of a wide variety of disorders. **The ingested infusions (consult with the doctor or specialist),** it can affect and **cause blood clots.** It can also **stunt growth (not scientifically proven).** Better to use in topical use, **especially and always, in under 12 years.**

- Common hawthorn, (Espino albar o Majuelo, en español)

Crataegus monogyna", also know as Single-seeded hawthorn, shrub originating to Europe, Asia and Africa. The leaves and flowers are used in cocoons, bark of young branches and drupes dried in the oven, mainly harvested in spring in the form of floral tops. It can be consumed in dry extract capsules and tinctures. To obtain results, a constant treatment is necessary at the rate of two cups of infusion per day. The cardiac symptoms begin to improve markedly from a month and a half of take. It is necessary to **suspend administration** if cardiac arrhythmias, drowsiness, stomach discomfort or abnormal sweating. **Use during pregnancy and breastfeeding, only under the supervision of a health professional. Contraindicated in hypertensive patients, in treatment with heteróxidos or Benzodiazepines.**

- Common lady's mantle, (Pie de león, en español)

"Alchemilla vulgaris", originally from Europe, it develops in grasslands and humid high mountain pastures where the climate is cold, low-rise plant. The flowering and the roots are those that have the active ingredients. **Before using ingested, consult a doctor.** Prepare with 1 dessert spoon per cup of water, boil 10 minutes, strain and drink up to 3 cups a day before eating. **Contraindicated children under 12 years, and persons with gastritis, gastroduodenal ulcer and heart disease.**

- Common poppy, (Amapola, en español)

"Papaver rhoeas", of unknown origin, but widespread in Eurasia and North Africa. The poppy seeds are very small and black, they bring incredible nutritional benefits and properties both curative and medicinal consumed regularly. It contains Omega 3 and ...**Continue on next page**

... Omega 6 fatty acids. Fiber (three tablespoons of poppy seeds provide 12% of the daily value of recommended dietary fiber). Vitamins of group B (especially B1, B2, B3, B5, B6 and folic acid or B9), as well as vitamin E and C., minerals such as Magnesium, Calcium, Manganese, Potassium, Phosphorus, Iron, Zinc and Copper. In the kitchen they are widely used for their versatility and flavor. They can be consumed in salads, soups, pasta or infusions. **For lack of knowledge in its effects, abstain pregnant, lactating, and children under 6 years.**

- Common soapwort, (Saponaria, en español)

"Saponaria officinalis", originating in central and southern Europe, it is very popular since the times of Dioscorides and Pliny. It stands out for its large buds and flowers of characteristic color. For medicinal uses internally, **use prepared preparations, as they do not contain toxic principles that harm/damage the stomach, intestine and kidneys.**

- Copalchi, (Copalchi, en español)

"Coutarea latífolia", plant originating in Mexico and Colombia, its crust is obtained Latiflora, active compound of **hypoglycemic properties, insulin vegetal, Improving the assimilation of carbohydrates.** The root is used mainly, but also the crust and leaves. **At reasonable doses is not toxic, follow instructions from medical personnel.**

- Corydalis cava, (Corydalis cava, en español)

"Corydalis cava", originally from Europe, from Portugal to the Caucasus. It contains properties such as Coridalina that exerts an inhibitory effect on the spinal cord, also alkaloids, especially those of the Aporfin that produce an effect similar to Morphine. Both act in a preanesthesia manner that does not alter the respiratory or circulatory functions. **It is used, under medical prescription, the fluid extract up to 2 gr. daily, maximum.**

- Cowslip primrose, (Hierba de san Pedro, en español)

"Primula officinalis" or "Primula veris", originating from Europe and Asia, it is edible and for seasoning. It has a stem with a lot of villi in all its extension of aroma quite unpleasant that spreads instantly. The infusion has a pleasant flavor. Very good balm, can be administered even in ...**Continue**

... childhood. **There are no known contraindications,** it is **recommended to consult** with the doctor or specialist.

- Cucumber, (Pepino, en español)

"Cucumis sativus", original from India, and cultivated for more than 3,000 years. Common vegetable that contains a variety of essential nutrients for the human body, and a lot of therapeutic effects on health. **It is not recommended in abundance to minors,** they may be more sensitive to present pictures of diarrhea or indigestion caused by this fruit. **It is not advisable to eat cucumbers to persons**: with indigestion or diarrea. **Plant of high diuretic value, abundant intake may cause some persons:** sensations of decay, muscular fatigue or decreased sexual appetite.

- Cumin, (Comino, en español)

"Cuminum cyminum", native to the Mediterranean basin, the seed of the fruit contains Cuminal, and various essential minerals such as Iron, Calcium and Magnesium, a spice with magnificent healing properties. Consumed in meals, sprinkled or infused (taste is not pleasant, can be mixed with other herbs or if you want to sweeten, see the sweeteners). **Contraindicated for children under 6 years, persons with Crohn's disease, irritable bowel syndrome, gastroduodenal ulcers, gastritis, ulcerative colitis, in case of epilepsy, Parkinson's, or any other neurological disease.**

Descriptions of plants letter D

- **Dandelion**
- **Devill´s backbone**
- **Devil´s claw**
- **Devil´s dung**
- **Deulkkae, see Perilla**
- **Dill**
- **Dong Quai, see Female ginseng**
- **Durmast oak**

- Dandelion, (Diente de león, en español)

"Taraxacum officinale", of European origin but extended to the rest of the orb, it is considered a weed by invasive. Magnificent depurative to clean the organism of the toxins accumulated by bad food, bad habits, sedentary lifestyle, etc. The most common way to use is in infusion, in poultices, or its fresh consumption in salads. **Do not use if you are taking antibiotics,** decrease their absorption. **Contraindicated in persons with stones or stones in the gallbladder, or kidneys, heartburn, reflux, stomach ulcers, allergies, those who take Lithium medicines or those used to increase the amounts of Potassium in the organism.**

- Devil's backbone, (Mayorca o Mayorga, en español)

"Pedilanthus tithymaloides", native of Mexico, Central America and the West Indies, of very old use. Milky juice bush, called in Cuba, Ítamo Real. Flowers pink or purple. Fruits in capsules, when dried open in three parts, with three seeds. For curative purposes the leaves are used (in infusion 10% per liter, **only in rinses, without swallowing), also its latex (diluted).** The root is abortive. **There are no known contraindications,** it is **recommended strongly to consult** with the doctor or specialist.

- Devil's claw, (Harpagofito, en español)

"Harpagophytum procumbens", native to southern Africa, the claved tuberous secondary roots are used, the usual use is in ingested infusion, in topical use and as a poultice or poultice. It exists in extract, tablets, capsules, creams, ointments, even the chopped root. **In very specific cases may appear:** symptoms of nausea, diarrhea or gastric discomfort. Monitor possible interaction with antiarrhythmic medications. **Use after meals and dosage according to specialist,** pulverizing, infusions, fluid or dry extract, tinctures, etc. They recommend infusion: 4.5 g / 300 ml. Take 100 ml every 8 hours. Fluid extract: 1: 1 (g / ml) 1.5 ml every 8 hours. Dry extract: 400 mg-800 mg a day. **Contraindicated in pregnancy or lactation women, patients with gastroduodenal ulcer, gastritis, obstruction of the biliary tract and irritable bowel.**

- Dill, in english, (Eneldo, en español)

"Anethum graveolens", originating from the mediterranean, in cold areas, very aromatic grass, both seeds and leaves are used. Being habitually used in fish stews to improve and accentuate its flavor. It is also used in infusion, and sprinkling on meals before serving. **Not recommended for in pregnancy or lactation women (only under medical supervision). Children under 12 years old, persons suffering from gastritis**

- Durmast oak, (Roble albar, en español)

"Querus petraea", originating from North Hemisphere, species that groups different species. The crust of the branches is used, although the leaves and the fruit are also used. The 3 mm thick spring crust is used. **Contraindicated in pregnancy or lactation women, and persons with medication that causes hepatotoxic damage.**

Descriptions of plants letter E

- **Eastern teaberry**
- **Edging lobelia**
- **Elms**
- **English primrose**
- **Escarole**
- **Estragon**
- **Evening primrose**
- **Evergreen oak**

- Eastern teaberry, (Gaulteria, en español)

"Gaultheria procumbens", plant originating in Mexico and north america, northeast of (USA) and Canada. Medicinal uses have been widely known for many centuries, especially by native Americans. Currently used in extract or oils. **Never ingest the essential oil.** The oil applied to the affected area is quickly absorbed by the skin. The methyl salicylate of the oil helps to numb the area and promote blood circulation providing a warm sensation. **Check** on the skin **before using** the essential oil, **in case it produces allergic reactions.**

- Edging lobelia, (Lobelia, en español)

"Lobelia erinus", originally from South Africa and introduced in Europe during the 18th century, it is used in infusions, ...**Continue on next page**

... gargles, powders, extracts, capsules. **Highly toxic plant. Only under medical prescription in controlled form and dosage. Do not prescribe simultaneously with medicines:** neuroleptics or others with alkaloids. **Contraindicated in pregnancy or lactation women and persons with hypertension.**

- Elms, (Olmo, en español)

"Ulmus minor" o "Ulmus carpinfolia", from the northern hemisphere of Eurasia and America. **It can cause:** hypersensitivity and contact allergy. **There are no known contraindications,** it is **recommended to consult** with the doctor or specialist.

- English primrose, (Oreja de oso, en español)

"Primula vulgaris", also know as Common primrose, originally from Europe, although they are also found in the Far East and Siberia. Often cultivated in Belarus, regions of St. Petersburg (Leningrad) and Kaliningrad. It uses the infusion of its flowers and leaves in moderate doses. **The excess causes:** vomiting, diarrhea, nausea, and other side effects. **Contraindicated in persons with acute renal/kidney diseases.**

- Escarole, (Escarola, en español)

"Cichorium inthybus var. Foliossum", its origin of wild chicory is believed. Also known as bitter chicory, both as plants developed from the commercialized endive (white-leaf escarole). Ancient civilizations soon discovered that this vegetable was keeping in its curly and tasty leaves a good number of properties for its high content of vitamin C, which favor the formation of collagen and red blood cells, increasing the absorption of iron and folic acid. The usual way to consume is in salads. **There are no known contraindications,** it is **recommended to consult** with the doctor or specialist.

- Estragon or Tarragon, (Estragón, en español)

"Artemisia dracunculus", of Asian origin, very appreciated in the kitchen for the flavor that it confers, as a culinary condiment it has practically no risk. **Consume in moderation and never daily:** pregnant (abortive and causing cramps/colic), people with diseases involving ...**Continue**

... the bowel, irritable bowel or Crohn's. **Essential oil is contraindicated, persons who are sick with cancer, lactation women (causing colic).**

- Evening primrose, (Onagra, en español)
"Oenothera", also know as Sundrops, originally from North America, native Indians used it for nutritional and medicinal purposes. In the XVIII century the Europeans considered it as a miraculous herb, its fruit has the shape like of a capsule. The essential oil is obtained after the cold pressing of the fruit, to be used in topical use or capsules. **3 pills** are consumed throughout the day **(follow the specialist's instructions).** The flowers can be used to aromatize certain salads. **The side effects could be:** headache, nausea and diarrhea. **Do not use for epileptics.**

- Evergreen oak, (Encina, en español)
"Quercus ilex", also know as Olm oak or Holly oak, tree that grows naturally in the Mediterranean basin. The bark/crust, flowers and leaves are the parts with medicinal qualities, with a large amount of tannins and other useful active ingredients, through infusions. **Contraindicated in pregnancy or lactation women, persons with iron deficiency anemia, constipation, gastritis, gastroduodenal ulcers, heart disease, fever.**

Descriptions of plants letter F

- Female ginseng
- Fennel
- Fragrant incense

- Fragrant incense, (Incienso aromático, en español)
"Plectranthus Madagascariensis Marginatus", also know as Plectranthus, original from india, tropical Africa and some Pacific islands, herb used as Ornament. It is a false incense, there are about 1,000 varieties of incense. **The essential oil is very toxic, it does not use in infusion, it has many risks, it can cause the death** in greater doses of **2gr. per liter in children, and 10 gr./ liter in adults.** Use only **burned or mixed with other aromatic plants.**

- Female ginseng, (Angélica china, en español)
"Angelica sinensis H", also know as Dong Quai, medicinal herb for multiple use for a wide variety of female pathologies, considered as **oriental viagra. The different parts of the root have different effects on health. Use only under medical or specialist prescription. Contraindicated in pregnancy or lactation women, persons with cancer of the uterus, breast and ovaries.**

- Fennel, (Hinojo, en español)
"Foeniculum vulgare", only one species of its kind, originating from Mediterranean coast where it grows in the wild. It is used as an infusion. **Contraindicated in patients with breast cancer or persons with hyperthyroidism. The essential oil its contraindicated in pregnancy or lactation women and under 6 years.**

Descriptions of plants letter G

- **Gallic rose, see Rose**
- **Garden angelica**
- **Garden nasturtium**
- **Garlic**
- **Gentius plant, see Illyrian king plant**
- **Geranium**
- **Ginger**
- **Ginkgo or Gingko**
- **Ginseng**
- **Goldenseal**
- **Gotu Kola, see Indian pennywort**
- **Grapevine / Grape**
- **Great morinda**
- **Great mullein**
- **Green coffe**
- **Green pepper**
- **Grenadia**
- **Ground elder**
- **Guarana**
- **Guatemalan indigo plant**

- Garden angelica, (Angélica, en español)
"Angelica archangelica", originating from northern Europe and Syria. Its leaves are used to flavor fruit compotes, jams, broths and liqueurs. Fresh leaves and stems are used in soups and salads. **Avoid sun exposure in your treatment. Contraindicated your ...Continue**

... essential oil internally during the pregnancy or lactation women, under 6 years, patients with epilepsy, Parkinson's or other neurological diseases. It is not recommended in any way in pregnancy or lactation women and diabetics.

- Garden nasturtium, (Capuchina, en español)

"Tropaeolum majus", originating from South America, perennial plant, crawling and climbing plant very striking for its flowers, is used to decorate gardens and outdoor spaces. In Europe it has acclimated in coastal areas as a wild plant. The whole plant is used, it has fleshy and branched stems, green leaves and yellow or red flowers. **Contraindicated in persons with hypothyroidism.**

- Garlic, (Ajo, en español)

"Allium sativum", probably of Asian origin, it has been cultivated for more than 7,000 years. Food of high nutritional value. Significantly reduces the toxicity of lead and associated symptoms. Consumed packaging to the brine does not cause halitosis and its intake is not annoying. **It can cause:** heartburn, flatulence or gas, belching, vomiting or diarrhea. **Avoid with food or anticoagulant supplements such as:** the Evening primrose oil, Grapefruit or Black willow. **Avoid also before or after surgery,** by decreasing the healing of wounds. **Excess consumption can cause problems:** in diabetics, bleeding or excessive anticoagulation. **Caution may interact with medications:** as anticoagulants, drugs for the heart, hypertension, contraceptives, corticosteroids, for cholesterol. **It is recommended not to take more than 2 cloves** of raw garlic on an empty stomach a day for persons with high or low blood pressure. **Contraindicated in pregnancy or lactation women, under 3 years, during menstruation, persons with hyperthyroidism.**

- Geranium or Cranesbills, (Geranio, en español)

"Pelargonium × hortorum", also know as Cranesbills, it's a hybrid with the Mallow, originating from Mediterranean basin, grows in all the temperate zones of the world with more than 400 species. Beautiful plant with very nice smell that it also serves to keep away ...**Continue on next page**

... mosquitoes pests in the garden. There are references to ancient Egypt in its use as a holistic treatment over time to improve physical, mental and emotional health. The different parts of the plant can be used in the form of oil: leaves, stems, roots, flowers. **Do not use the oil ingested in children under 6 years.**

- Ginger, (Jengibre, en español)

"Zingiber officinale", originating from Asia and East for the USA, tuber of spicy flavor covered with brown skin. It is a sensational plant also as an ingredient widely used in gastronomy. Traditionally, ginger has been and it is one of the most popular plants in traditional Chinese medicine. It can be used sprinkled, as an ingredient in stews or in infusion (masking, can be unpleasant). **Contraindicated in pregnancy or lactation women, diabetics, persons with gallstones, gastritis, gastroduodenal ulcers, irritable colon, colitis, Crohn's disease, in treatment with medicines for blood circulation, anticoagulants, or against the hypertension.**

- Ginkgo or Gingko, (Ginkgo biloba, en español)

"Ginkgophyta", tree originating in China, Darwin called it "living fossil". The extract of the leaves is considered an effective natural remedy, is used as an infusion with 50 grams of dried leaves in 500 milliliters of water and drink about three cups per day. **Do not consume the seeds, they are very toxic.** There are pills and extracts, **the extract in excess can cause:** skin problems and headache. **Contraindicated in pregnancy or lactation women under 6 years, diabetic, hypertensive, epileptic, consuming AAS (aspirin), anticoagulant medications or before a surgical intervention.**

- Ginseng, (Ginseng, en español)

"Panax ginseng", also know as Korean ginseng or Chinese ginseng, it grows in high areas of Asia from Russia, and in North America from Mexico. It is one of the best known medicinal plants in the world. The root is used, whose components increase brain activity, but not nervous excitement. On the other hand, it improves the performance and the physical resistance. It is recommended to take one to three 500 mg tablets in the morning, after breakfast, **for four or six weeks and rest for two months.** It exists in different presentations, ...**Continue**

... for infusions, in pills, supplements, sweets/candies, etc. **Contraindicated in pregnancy or lactation women, children under 12 years, persons with insomnia, migraines, headaches, hypertension, varicose veins, heart disease, hyperthyroidism and hypothyroidism, diabetics, with autoimmune diseases such as lupus or rheumatoid arthritis, and persons with organ transplants.**

- Goldenseal, (Hydrastis o Sello de oro, en español)

"Hydrastis canadensis", of the most popular sold in the American market. Since 1798 its medicinal virtues are known, it has recently gained a reputation as an herbal antibiotic and immune system enhancer. **Use only under medical or specialist prescription**. The color of its rhizome and some brands remember old stamps to seal letters. It is also found as balsam, tincture, powder and tablets. **Contraindicated in pregnancy or lactation women, children under 12 years, persons with hypertension or with heart problems.**

- Grapevine / Grape, (Vid / Uva, en español)

"Vitis vinífera", the origin of grapes grown in Europe is believed to be in the Caspian Sea region. For curative remedies the leaves, fruits and oil extracted from the seeds are used. In topical use what is known as "water or sap of vine shoots or red vine" is very appropriate. It is the sap of the plant that is obtained in spring, usually in the month of March before the leaves come out. A tender branch is cut and a liquid is allowed to distill through the cut and collect in a very clean glass. **Do not use** dosage **forms with alcohol content in under 6 years or persons with ethyl** problems. **There are no known contraindications,** it is **recommended to consult** with the doctor or specialist.

- Great morinda, (Noni, en español)

"Morinda citrifolia", also know as Noni, a fruit originating in the Polynesian islands, used by the natives to cure most diseases, is consumed directly or in juice. **Contraindicated in pregnancy or lactation women, persons transplanted, affected by heart failure, who take oral anticoagulants, with control of potassium in their diet and terminal renal patients.**

- Great mullein or Mullein, (Gordolobo, en español)

"Verbascum thasur", originating in Europe and North Africa. **Its use may interfere with medications and enhance the action of anticoagulants. The essential oil is contraindicated in persons with ruptured eardrums. Essential oil and ingested infusion are contraindicated in pregnancy or lactation women,**

- Green coffe, (Café verde, en español)

Also called Nescafé, it is coffee without toasting, its consumption has been analyzed in numerous clinical studies where it is demonstrated that the utilities and **therapeutic properties are similar to Coffee, with the advantage that it does not cause** headaches, nausea, insomnia and respect to dependence, quite the contrary, is recommended for different types of addictions. **Indecipherable flavor and smell** (camouflage with a few drops of vanilla, Mint or other aromatic plant). **Contraindicated in pregnancy and children under 12 years, patients with renal/kidney, cardiac, hypertensive, gastroduodenal or gastritis problems, and persons sensitive to caffeine.**

- Green pepper, (Pimiento verde, en español)

"Capsicum annuum", originating from America, being known in Europe by the Spanish in the 16th century, it is the most immature of peppers, bitter taste with half of vitamin C and a tenth of vitamin A compared to red or yellow color. Powerful antioxidant, vitamin C is necessary for proper absorption of iron if deficient. The green pepper is among the lowest calorie foods, 100 gr. contains only 19.68 kcal. **There are no known contraindications,** it is **recommended to consult** with the doctor or specialist.

- Grenadia, (Granadilla, en español)

"Passiflora ligularis", also know as Sweet granadilla, climbing plant of the Andes, domesticated in the pre-Inca era. Type of passion fruit whose pulp is full of hard blackish seeds, surrounded by a light gray transparent gelatinous ring and aromatic acid flavor, it is recommended to **integrate the baby** as one of the first foods. **As side effects we can cite:** nausea, vomiting, abdominal pain and diarrhea, due to excesive ...**Continue**

... consumption. **Contraindicated to allergy sufferers, in persons diabetics** (due to its high content of sugars), **in hepatics or with a diet** (due to its caloric intake).

- Ground elder, (Podagraria, en español)

"Aegopodium podagraria", originally from Europe, **considered a weed,** it is invasive and expands territorially forming a bush that spreads over other species in a wild form. It is edible in salads or stews. The usual is the infusion with dried leaves, use 15 gr. for each cup of boiling water, rest a few minutes, filter and drink up to 2 cups a day. **Contraindicated in pregnancy or lactation women, and children under 12 years.**

- Guarana, (Guaraná, en español)

"Paullinia cupana", originally from northern Brazil. **It is not recommended before bedtime,** caffeine can lead to insomnia. It's an excellent tonic, sold in capsules and beverages. **Contraindicated in pregnancy, persons that consume Ephedrine, with cardiovascular diseases, hypertension, kidney/renal disease, hyperthyroidism and anxiety disorders and children under 6 years.**

- Guatemalan indigo plant, (Índigo o Añil, en español)

"Indigófera suffruticosa", originally from the American tropics, in Peru it is distributed along the coast and the Amazon, a wild plant that grows from sea level to 1,100 m. **Overdose as a purgative may present severe diarrhea and spasms.** Considered a **toxic plant.** It is commonly used in powders. **Better to use ointments already prepared. Contraindicated in pregnancy or lactation women.**

Descriptions of plants letter H

- Hazel
- Hazelnut
- Heath speedwell
- Heater, see
  Briar root
- Helychrysum
- Henna
- Herb Bennet
- Herb of grace,
  see Rue

- Hogweed
- Holly oak, see
  Evergreen oak
- Honeysuckle
- Hops
- Horehound
- Horseradish
- Huan qin, see
  Baikal skullcap
- Hypericum, see
  Perforate St John's-wort

- Hazel, (Avellano, en español)

"Corylus avellana", tree native to the Mediterranean. It uses the infusions of crusts and leaves ingested or in topical use (washed and in compresses), **Contraindicated in persons with gastritis and gastroduodenal ulcer (may cause discomfort and constipation).**

- Hazelnut, (Avellana, en español)

Fruit of the tree "Corylus avellana", natural source of protein and an excellent source of energy easily assimilable by our organism, rich in fat, about 70%, with proteins and carbohydrates. **Very suitable for celiacs** as it does not contain gluten. **You just have to take into account, allergy or intolerance to nuts.**

- Heath speedwell, (Verónica, en español)

"Veronica officinalis", also know as Common gypsyweed, very common and abundant climbing herb in the mountainous places of Europe and throughout America. For the curative remedies the whole plant is used, without the roots, usually in infusion for internal and topical use. Ingested is recommended pour 1 teaspoon of dessert with herbs in ¼ liter of boiling water. Rest 10 minutes, strain and take 1 to 3 times a day, warm. For topical use as rinses, gargles, poultices, washes, boil 40 gr. per liter of water for 10 minutes, strain use. **There are no known contraindications,** it is **recommended to consult** with the doctor or specialist.

- Helychrysum, (Helicriso, en español)

"Helichrysum stoechas", wild plant that grows in the Mediterranean basin of rocky areas and dry soils. With dense bouquets of small flowers that are used internally or in topical use (washes, compresses). ...**Continue**

... There are different presentations for infusion, extracts, syrup and ointments. **Its essential oil is neurotoxic, only used in topical use. Contraindicated in pregnancy or lactation women, persons taking:** anticoagulants or drugs of opposite effect, in case of taking corticoids or **with obstructions of the biliary tract.**

- Henna, (Henna, en español)

"Lawsonia inermis", shrub of African origin also know as Mehandi, Panwar, Shudi. It lowers the temperature of the human body, custom in the Arab world to refresh itself. It is used in powder (of seeds) for meals or in infusion. **Contraindicated in any modality, in pregnant women (abortive), or lactation, and children under 6 years.**

- Herb Bennet, (Cariofilada, en español)

"Geum urbanum", It grows in shady places like the edges of the forests of Europe and Asia. It is used, rhizomes (before flowering) and leaves (in bloom). **This plant should not be used with iron containers. Contraindicated ingested persons with gastritis or gastroduodenal ulcers.**

- Hogweed, (Branca ursina, en español)

"Heracleum sphondylium", it grows in many regions of central and southern Europe. The whole plant is used for its properties as hypotensive, tonic, depurative, stimulant and digestive. **Sun exposure to body parts treated with the fresh plant can cause painful skin eruptions and blisters (photosensitization).**

- Honey, (Miel, en español)

Another exception to this book is mentioned as being produced by bees from flowers. Food advised to strengthen our immune system, excellent natural option for its antibacterial and antimicrobial qualities. **Not suitable for:** diabetics, persons with a diet to lose weight, (there are exceptions). **Contraindicated in under 1 year, may contain spores, cause of Botulism and Allergies.**

- Honeysuckle, (Madreselva, en español)

"Lonicera xylosteum" or "Lonicera caprifolium", originating from Europe, there are three edible species, north, south and central Europe, also those of Altai and Kamchatka (both in Russia). There are 14 species of wild honeysuckle. Because of its detoxifying action, **fresh shoots are used to treat mushroom poisoning.** The usual use is the infusions of the crust, or of the white flowers (they grow together with the yellow ones). There are also elaborated syrups. **The main edible difference of the berries is the color,** the almost **black or blue color, you can eat,** but the **orange or red tones are poisonous.**

- Hops, (Lúpulo, en español)

"Humulus lupulus", originating from Europe, Western Asia and North America, it is a plant that is easily recognized by the peculiarity of being climber and whose stems are always rolled to the right, grows near rivers or areas with humidity. In some persons, **flowers can cause contact dermatitis.** For medicinal remedies can use ingested or in topical use the infusion of flowers or grains, also in juice. **In excessive doses can cause:** nausea and vomiting. **The pregnancy or lactation women, before consuming, consult with the doctor or specialist.**

- Horehound, (Marrubio, en español)

"Marrubium vulgare", also know as White horehound, originating from Europe and North Africa, plant with numerous villi that give off a pleasant aroma very similar to apples. Grows wild in abandoned places or along the edges on roads or paths, at the foot of walls, on vacant lots, among rubble, etc. The leaves and branches are used in infusion, is prepared by pouring in 200 ml of boiling water, a teaspoon of Horehound and some Mint about 3 minutes more. Rest a few minutes, strain and drink immediately, two to three cups a day 10 minutes after meals. They are sold in capsules and tincture **Contraindicated in pregnancy women.**

- Horseradish, (Rábano rusticano, en español)

"Armoracia rusticana", originally from Russia and south-west Asia, it is increasingly rare to have abandoned its cultivation. **It is used commercially in very strong mustards to be extremely spicy, ...Continue on nex page**

... can irritate the digestive tract and cause vomiting of blood or diarrhea, the usual form is the root grated ingested or as a poultice.

Descriptions of plants letter I

- Ice-cream-bean
- Illyrian king plant
- Indian fig opuntia
- Indian ginseng, see Ashwagandha
- Indian gooseberry
- Indian Lotus, see lotus
- Indian pennywort
- Indian sandalwood
- Ivy

- Ice-cream-bean, (Guamá, en español)

"Inga edulis", there are more than 300 species, the one described here is called Ingá o Pacae, tree native to Central and South America, grows close to rivers and lakes, its pods are edible and therapeutic properties. **There are no known contraindications,** it is **recommended to consult** with the doctor or specialist.

- Illyrian king plant or Gentius plant, (Genciana, en español)

"Gentiana", native of the Carpathians, is hardly found in other mountain ranges of Europe and Asia, is in danger of extinction, unscrupulous collectors have put at risk because this plant takes time to grow. Medicinal herb capable of stimulating digestive glandular cells, its medicinal properties transform it into a **plant that stimulates the immune system** by favoring the growth of the number of leukocytes or white cells of the immune system. The roots are used for their medicinal properties in tinctures. **Contraindicated during lactating mothers, and persons with gastroduodenal ulcer.**

- Indian fig opuntia or Nopal, (Chumbera o Nopal, en español)

"Opuntia ficus-indica", cactus native to the arid and dry lands of northern Mexico, cactus juice is used to treat a number of inflammatory conditions. In spring they develop in delicious ...**Continue on next page**

... cactus fruits shaped like prickly pear, called Tuna, contain nutrients and antioxidants, such as vitamins C, E, A, Iron, Calcium, **Carotenoids, Flavonoids, with natural anti-inflammatory properties.** Studies estimate that in the future it could **provide new treatments in chronic inflammatory diseases,** where prostaglandins play an important role in cases of asthma, allergies, dermatitis, arthritis, migraines and psoriasis. Its properties reduce the symptoms of hangover by reducing the organic inflammation by high alcohol intake. **As side effects includes:** diarrhea, nausea, abdominal fullness, headache and increased volume and frequency of bowel movements. It consumes its fruits or the extracts of the plant, being the recommended dose, two capsules of Nopal with a glass of water before the meals. **It is basically used in forms of ointments or extracts.** A syrup is made with its fruit called Tuna syrup. **A lot of caution in patients with diabetes or low blood sugar, high cholesterol, low blood pressure or thyroid dysfunction. Contraindicated in pregnancy or lactation women.**

- Indian gooseberry, (Amla o Grosella espinosa, en español)

"Phyllanthus emblica", also know as Amla, Amalaki or Chiratya (indian term) to be native to India. Clinical trials demonstrated their spectacular health benefits, **healthy persons as sick can eat it daily,** in prevention and treatment, as fresh or canned fruit. There is a dry extract, capsules, pills, the usual doses vary from 400 mg / day to 3,000 mg / day. The fluid extract is taken between 0.6-1 g. day. The most common way to consume is the infusion, made between 30 to 60 gr. per liter of water. **There are no known contraindications,** it is **recommended to consult** with the doctor or specialist.

- Indian pennywort, (Hidrocotyle, en español)

"Hydrocotyle", originally from India and China, widely used for 3,000 years in the Orient, with different names such as: Gotu Kola or Kola. Its dry or fresh leaves and its roots are used for healing purposes. In general, in 2 or 3 weeks of treatment, very good results are achieved. **In high doses (for its essential oil) is:** narcotic, presenting headaches, vertigo, hypertension, respiratory failure. **In topical use caution** persons with cutaneous hypersensitivity. **There are several presentations and ...Continue**

... forms such as: infusions, drops, tablets, gels, lotions, soaps, facial and body creams, powdered extract. It can even be consumed in dishes of oriental origin. **Consult with the doctor or specialist, before possible interactions with:** medication of antidepressants or benzodiazepines. **Contraindicated in pregnancy, in fertility treatment, or lactation women, under 6 years, diabetics, hepatic, people with high cholesterol or renal failure.**

- Indian sandalwood, (Árbol del sándalo, en español)
"Santalum álbum", originally from India, considered a "sacred tree" and protected. It is used to massage with your oil diluted at 1% maximum with sweet almond oil, **in non-allergic persons is safe.** Use with **caution patients with fungal infections** on the skin, scalp and nails, also by **persons in treatment with anxiolytics. Contraindicated in pregnancy, or lactation women.**

- Ivy, (Hiedra, en español)
"Hedera hélix", Perennial-leaf climbing plant widely used for medicinal purposes, and one of the scarce survivors in Europe of the Tertiary-era Laurisilva flora. **It can produce:** allergic rhinitis sensitization and symptoms of both respiratory and skin allergies. **Its fruits are toxic and can cause vomiting and diarrhea.** The most common way to use is in decoctions. **Contraindicated in pregnancy or lactation women. There is a toxic (American) variety.**

Descriptions of plants letter J

- Jamaica pepper
- Jamaican dogwood
- Japanese pagoda tree
- Jasmine
- Jessamine, see Yellow jessamine

- Jamaica pepper, (Pimienta de Jamaica, en español)
"Pimenta dioica", also know as Allspice, of the tree that grows in Jamaica, Mexico, Guatemala and Belize, and Pepper that is not, is actually a berry that collects green and dried in the sun and ...**Continue on next page**

... when dried in the sun it takes its characteristic brown color. Once dry they remember large peppers and hence their name, but it does not itch. The oil essential it can irritate the skin in very sensitive persons, to avoid, try for the first time in small quantities. **It is not recommended in pregnancy or lactation women due to insufficient scientific evidence available.**

- Jamaican dogwood, (Guamá candelón, en español)

"Piscidia piscipula", native to Mexico, Cuba, Jamaica, Martinique, Brazil, and coastal areas of the Caribbean. **Do not drink alcohol during treatment with this plant.** The root crust is used, in tincture or fluid extract. **Contraindicated in pregnancy or lactation women, under 12 years, Parkinson's patients, or with medications that affect the nervous system.**

- Jasmine, (Jazmín, en español)

"Jasminum", aromatic flower coveted for its exquisite perfume, jasmine tea is the most consumed in China for centuries. There are 300 varieties, some with yellow flowers. The flowers are used for therapeutic purposes, mainly in infusion with green tea, although it can be made with others according to taste. **Pregnancy, lactation women moderate doses of jasmine with no side effects** or harmful. **Consumed in excess, may have side effects such as:** anxiety, insomnia, dizziness, palpitations.

- Japanese pagoda tree, (Sófora, en español)

"Styphnolobium japonicum", originally from East Asia who was transferred to Japan (known as Japan's Acacia). Popular tree in the northern regions for its white flowers blooming at the end of summer, very widespread in bonsai. **Any treatment and dosage will only be under medical or specialist prescription.** For medicinal uses different parts of the tree are used, depending on the ailment to be treated, and in different ways: tinctures, dust/powder, pills, infusions, of the plant and the fruit. **Excessive doses, or very prolonged use can produce symptoms of intoxication such as:** paralysis and spasms, even reaching respiratory arrest. **Contraindicated in pregnancy or lactation women.**

Descriptions of plants letter K

- Kalonchoe
- Kava or Kava-Kava
- Kinkeliba
- Kola, see
  Indian pennywort
- Korean ginseng,
  see Ginseng
- Kiwi
- Kudzu

- Kalonchoe, (Kalonchoe o Espinazo del diablo, en español)

"Kalanchoe daigremontiana", commonly called Devil´s backbone or Mother of thousands, originally from Madagascar. The genus Kalanchoe comprises some 125 species of the Crassulaceae family. **It should not be used for long periods of time** if it is not for treatment. Take a **maximum of 5 gr. per kilo of the person to be treated, and day.** Acid-flavored leaves, **the infusion** is prepared with 30 gr. Fresh leaf in 3 shots a day (before each meal). Add water from your juice to give more volume to the infusion. You can **eat raw** in salads. There are fluid extracts. **Consult with the doctor** persons with heart disease. **Contraindicated in pregnancy (abortive).**

- Kava or Kava-Kava, (Kava, en español)

"Piper methysticum", plant of Polynesia, the root is used, so calming effects that it has been compared with the Valium, without producing harmful or secondary effects used intelligently. **Consuming with caution, being a toxic plant,** in high doses **could cause** a state of **"drunkenness"** similar to alcohol, affecting reasoning, coordination and eloquence. **Contraindicated in pregnancy, liver and kidney patients, or people with medications for anxiety or depression.**

- Kinkeliba, (Combreto, en español)

"Combretum micranthum", native of central Africa, its use is recommended after meals. **Dosage under medical prescription. High doses cause:** vomiting, acidity, gastritis, and gastroduodenal ulcers. The sheets are used in different forms that are sold in specialized stores. **Contraindicated in pregnancy or lactation women, under 6 years, and the elderly.**

- Kiwi, (Kiwi, en español)

"Actinidia deliciosa", originating from China, are many its properties and benefits due to the nutrients it provides. **Because of its potassium content, it should be taken into account by persons with renal insufficiency and those who require special controlled diets in this mineral.**

- Kudzu, (Kudzu en español)

"Pueraria lobata", also know as East Asian arrowroot, originating from China, from its roots you get an extremely popular ingredient in Japan, known for its delicate texture, **It does not contain gluten,** ideal for coeliacs, and very easy to digest. In the kitchen it is used as a thickener, a teaspoon of kudzu equivalent to two tablespoons of wheat flour or a tablespoon of cornmeal. You can also drink. **There are no known contraindications,** it is **recommended to consult** with the doctor or specialist.

Descriptions of plants letter L

- **Lamb´s lettuce**
- **Larch tree**
- **Lemon balm**
- **Lemon verbena**
- **Lemon**
- **Lice-Bane**
- **Linden tree**
- **Lingzhi mushroom, see Reishi mushroom**
- **Lotus**
- **Lovage**
- **Luma chequen, see White Chilean myrtle**

- Lamb´s lettuce, (Canónigo, en español)

"Valerianella locusta", originating in Europe, Asia Minor and the Caucasus, grows spontaneously in meadows and meadows, prairies with humidity, and rarely outside of Europe. Emphasizes its alphalinolenic acid (ALA), very scarce in the vegetable kingdom, and of tiny calories, it can be eaten in salads (more usual) or cooked. Very smooth flavor, with a certain dry fruit flavor and properties similar to Valerian. **There are no known contraindications,** it is **recommended to consult** with the doctor or specialist.

- Larch tree, (Alerce, en español)

"Fitzroya cupressoides", also know as Patagonian cypress tree, originating in the southern cone of America, a millennial tree and one of the oldest on the planet, of light wood, rot-resistant, brown or reddish brown. Its leaves expel a liquid used to sweeten. For the ailments the inner crust of the trunk is used. **Use only under medical prescription.**

- Lavender, (Lavanda, en español)

"Lavandula angustifolia", originating from Mediterranean, bush of showy violet or bluish flowers in the shape of spikes, with a characteristic and pleasant aroma. The flowers are used as an essential oil or in infusion. **In topical use it is recommended to dilute the oil,** heat where it is applied, sometimes it can hurt babies and children.

- **The infusion, do not use for the following pathologies:** epilepsy, gastritis, Crohn's disease, irritable bowel syndrome, liver disease, neurological, Parkinson's, colitis.
- **Essential oil,** in breathing problems from a cold, it is applied to the skin near the neck or chest, relaxes the muscles around the application area allowing proper breathing. **May worsen symptoms of disease:** irritable bowel syndrome, colitis, Crohn's disease, diarrhea, digestive system, headache and muscle, abdominal swelling and blood in the stool. **Contraindicated with dermatitis, in pregnancy or lactation women and under 6 years.**

- Lemon, (Limón, en español)

"Citrus × limón", originally from Northeast Asia, introduced in Europe through Spain by the Arabs, fruit with multiple properties especially taken on an empty stomach, is more digestible and less harmful dissolved in wáter. **In large quantities could cause:** heartburn, upset stomach, nausea, headache, diarrhea. It affects the dental enamel exposing it to cavities (better to drink with a straw). **Contraindicated during the first 3 months of pregnancy, and during lactating mothers, people sick with gastritis, peptic ulcers, anemia, rickets, demineralization, bone decalcification, gingivitis, sores and cracks in the mouth or tongue.**

- **Lemon balm,** (Melisa, en español)

"Melissa officinalis", also know as Melissa, endemic plant of the Mediterranean coast, aromatic, with a certain smell of lemon. **Contraindicated the essential oil orally.** The most common use is infusion. **Inadequate doses can produce:** gastroenteritis, nausea, vomiting and abdominal pain. **Do not use with:** synthetic antidepressants, antihistamines, narcotics, or other sedatives. **Contraindicated in persons with hypothyroidism.**

- **Lemon verbena,** (Cedrón o Hierbaluisa, en español)

"Aloysia citriodora", shrub originating from South America where it grows wild, was introduced in Europe in the 17th century. Its leaves are used in infusion. **Contraindicated in pregnancy or lactation women and persons with thyroid.**

- **Lice-Bane or Stavesacre,** (Estafisagria, en español)

"Delphinium staphisagria", originally from the Mediterranean basin. **Poisonous plant, use only preparations under medical control.** Sometimes it is useful to use it simultaneously in topical usage on ulcers, herpes, etc. The dosage is carried out **(under medical or specialist control),** with one part of the tincture by ten of water. **Under strict medical control,** during menstruation. **Contraindicated in pregnancy or lactation women.**

- **Linden tree,** (Árbol de Tilo, en español)

"Tilia platyphyllos", also know as Large-leaved linden, it grows in Europe, Asia, America and exceptionally in cold and humid regions of the northern hemisphere, in Russia they form large forest areas. It is one of the most important medicinal plants, it is used mainly the infusion of flowers, dry bracts, crust and sapwood (white part of under the crust of the tree). **It is convenient to see Tila tree,** when sharing remedies. **It is also used as an antidote,** in case of ingesting toxic substances. **Consult with the doctor, pregnancy or lactation women, heart patients, with stomach pains unknown.**

- Lotus or Indian lotus, (Loto, en español)

"Nelumbo nucifera", also know as Indian Lotus, of the same species as the Water Lily, but different plants, the Water Lily is at rest on the water, the Lotus seems to emerge from it. Original from the Middle East, the flower barely lasts a few days, and exhales a special perfume. To take advantage of its properties you can consume: the flower, the rhizome (or root), seeds and even the leaves to make light soups. The raw and previously cut rhizome is eaten as is and brings a sophisticated and fresh note to greasy dishes. There is essence (very expensive). From the dried root is made a very popular infusion that can be consumed alone or mixed with other herbs like green tea. **Do not take 2 weeks before a surgical intervention.** As side effects might include: **flatulence, constipation, gastrointestinal irritations.** Decreased **blood pressure and antiarrhythmic activity** (to treat abnormal heart beats) **and contraceptive.** At **risk of bleeding** may cause your increase. **Contraindicated in pregnant or lactation women** (due to lack of scientific evidence). **Diabetic patients with hemorrhagic disorders, constipation and stomach distention (swelling).**

- Lovage, (Levístico o Apio del monte, en español)

"Levisticum officinale", originally from central Asia, extended to the coastal countries of the Western Mediterranean. The roots are mainly used (of arómatico smell) and to a lesser extent their leaves, seeds and the young stems in infusion, exists in tinctures. The fresh plant can produce contact dermatitis (furocoumarins). It can be used as a culinary condiment. To make the infusion use one tablespoon of coffee per cup, boil 5 minutes and take 2 or 3 times a day. **The use of your oil is counterproductive with kidney/renal failure. It can cause discomfort and dizziness. Contraindicated during pregnancy. Contraindicated as a diuretic in the presence of hypertension, heart disease or renal failure, use only by prescription and under medical supervision.**

Descriptions of plants letter M

- Maca
- Magnolia-vine
- Manioc, see Cassava
- Marjoram
- Marsh skullcap
- Martagon lily
- Maypop, see Passionflower
- Mayten
- Melon, see Muskmelon
- Melissa, see Lemon balm
- Meridian fennel
- Mexican pepperleaf
- Mignonette tree
- Mimosa, see Silver wattle
- Mint
- Mistletoe
- Motherwort
- Muira puama
- Mullein, see Great mullein
- Muskmelon
- Muskroot, see Sumbal

- Maca, (Maca, en español)

"Lepidium meyenii", native to the Andes of Peru and Bolivia, cultivated in the Peruvian Andes for almost 2,600 years. **At the beginning of taking maca, you can experience:** insomnia and hyperactivity, although they can be symptoms of detoxification. It is advisable to eat alone with water or mixing it with vegetables, soups or broths between **1 and 3 tablespoons of dust/powder per day.** If taken daily, it is advisable to **free one day each week. Contraindicated in pregnancy or lactation women, or consult** with the doctor or specialist.

- Magnolia-vine, (Schizandra, en español)

"Schisandra chinensis", originally from northern China, it is also called the fruit of the five flavors, its Chinese name is Wu-Wei-Zi. The berries have been used in traditional Chinese medicine for more than 2,000 years, one of the few herbs that contains the three treasures known as Jing, Qi and Shen (essence, energy and spirit). It is marketed in the form of tea, drops and capsules. Advise as appropriate dose are 450 mg, 3 times a day. **Better to follow specialist instructions.** It can produce: acidity, stomach pain and decreased appetite. **Do not consume due to increased ...Continue**

... **sleepiness with:** Lorazepam, Diazepam, Phenobarbital, Codeine, Ibuprofen, Naxoproxene and antidepressants. **Contraindicated in pregnancy or lactation women, and persons with gastrointestinal disorders.**

- Marjoram, (Mejorana, en español)

"Origanum majorana", originating from Eastern Mediterranean basin, its used to Provencal herbs, with an aroma similar to oregano. **Fresh can cause irritation of the eyes and skin.** The usual use is in infusion, three cups a day. **Contraindicated in pregnancy or lactation women, under 6 years, persons with problems of hematuria (blood in the urine), gastroduodenal ulcers, hepatic, gastritis, Crohn's disease, irritable bowel syndrome, Parkinson's, and neurological diseases.**

- Marsh skullcap, (Escutelaria azul, en español)

"Scutellaria galericulata", native of the European and American Northern Hemisphere, plant of violet and blue flowers in the shape of a bell. It uses stems leaves and flowers in infusion, although there are capsules. **It can cause side effects such as:** drowsiness, confusion and lightheadedness. **Contraindicated in pregnancy or lactation women.**

- Martagon Lily, (Martagón, en español)

"Lilium martagon", also know as Turk´s cap Lily, plant of oriental origin that although it extends from Portugal to Mongolia, usually grows in mountainous areas between Beech, Oak, Evergreen oak / Olm oak / Holly oak forest. **Gives off a strong smell** that can cause **dizziness in some persons.** The infusion of stems, bulbs, leaves and flowers (there are pink and White color) is usually used. It is prepared with a bulb of approximately 15 gr. pour boiling water and put in infusion for 15 minutes, strain and take three times a day. **There are no known contraindications,** it is **recommended to consult** with the doctor or specialist.

- Mayten, (Maitén, en español)

"Maytenus boaria", tree originally from Chile, the Mapuche people used this plant as purgative and against poisons. It serves as an antidote to cure the skin rashes produced by the Litre disease. ...**Continue on next page**

... You can prepare infusions with dried leaves and seeds, another highly recommended option is to use it to make steam or washed with them for external use. **Caution people with sensitive stomachs or when the presence of intestinal diseases is suspected.**

- Meridian fennel, (Alcaravea, en español)

"Carum carvi", also know as Caraway, originally from Europe, West Asia and North Africa. The Romans and ancient Greeks did not use or hardly knew. Alcarvea is a word of Arabic origin, used in Spain since 1,400. It is used for medicinal purposes its seeds, very similar to cumin, which come from a plant similar to the Carrot. **As a side effect** it can produce stomach acidity. **In large doses and in prolonged periods, it can damage:** the kidneys and the liver. **Essential oil can cause:** dizziness, convulsions and headaches. **Check with your doctor before using, pregnancy or lactation women.**

- Mexican pepperleaf, (Yerba santa, en español)

"Piper auritum", shrub native to Mesoamerica, the leaf has a heart shape, are aromatic, sweet and somewhat spicy. It is used in infusion, in poultices and in tincture. It is also usually added in small pieces to certain Tamales. **Consult with the doctor or specialist before using: pregnancy or lactation women, under xx years and and patients with severe kidney or liver disease.**

- Mignonette tree, (Reseda, en español)

"Reseda lutea", native of Eurasia to Pakistan, Africa, Macronesia, can be found in North America introduced but considered undergrowth. Plant widely used as a dye, being rich in Luteolin, which produces a bright yellow color. **There are no known contraindications,** it is **recommended to consult** with the doctor or specialist.

- Mint, (Menta, en español)

"Mentha", millenary plant that is found in all continents, is similar to Spearmint and composed mainly of water, fiber, proteins, minerals, vitamins and amino acids. Menthol or Pippermint is extracted from the essential oil of mint, with it a type of alcohol discovered ...**Continue**

... thousands of years ago is elaborated in Japan. **Mint piperita** is usually sold, a sterile hybrid obtained from the crossing of the aquatic Mint and Spearmint, but with the same properties as the Mint. **Do not abuse the consumption of Menthol, it worsens the symptoms in persons with:** digestive ulcers, hiatus hernia or heartburn. **Contraindicated essential oils (Menthol) in pregnancy or lactation women, persons with hepatic pathologies, ulcerative colitis or diarrhea.**

- Mistletoe, (Muérdago, en español)

"Viscum álbum", **parasitic and toxic plant,** rooted on other plants and trees, such as Pine. Sacred plant for the Druids of the traditional Celtic culture, In the comics of Asterix and Obelix there are continuous references to it. **Protected species, not collect indiscriminately,** the berries of Mistletoe not to be ingested, neither in very low doses, it can produce very serious nervous and cardiac alterations, **there are elaborated products to use only under medical supervision.** The root, leaves and young branches are used in the remedies, usually in the form of injectables. **Do not use dosage forms with alcohol content by persons with ethyl problems. Contraindicated in pregnancy or lactation women, under 16 years, and persons with heart disease, kidney failure, liver diseases.**

- Motherwort, (Agripalma, en español)

"Leonorus cardiaca", plant native to Asia and North America. **In large quantities, it leads to:** unpayable thirst, belly aches, bloody stools/feces and vomiting. Monitor interaction with digitalis, laxative or diuretic treatments. **Contraindicated in pregnancy women, under 2 years.**

- Muira puama, (Muira puama, en español)

"Ptychopetalum olacoides", it is located in the Amazon rainforest. Its root and crust are used by the indigenous peoples of Río Negro (South America) to treat a wide variety of diseases, different forms of preparations are sold. **Do not consume under treatment with:** allopathic psychotropic drugs, antidepressants, anxiolytics or tranquilizers. **Contraindicated in pregnancy or lactation women, under 12 years and persons hypertensive.**

- Muskmelon or Melon, (Melón, en español)

"Cucumis melo", of uncertain origin of Central Asia or Africa. It grows in warm climates and not very humid with lots of light. There are many varieties: **Toad skin** (the most common, crust, greenish and rough, whitish pulp), **Gaul or Galia** (somewhat rough skin yellowish-green and with stretch marks, yellowish-white pulp), **Yellow, Cantaloupe or Spanspek** (somewhat rough skin of a greenish color, orange pulp), **Honeydew** (green or orange pulp). **Tendral** (dark green crust), **Rochet** (yellowish-white pulp). **Contraindicated the excess in pregnancy or lactation women, under 6 years, patients with diabetes, or persons with vesicular problems, anorexia, stress, anxiety.**

- Myrrh, (Mirra en español)

"Commiphora myrrha", also know as African myrrh, originating from Somalia and African regions. It grows in the Middle East. To prepare the infusion use 1 to 2 teaspoons of well-sprayed Myrrh herb and the equivalent of a cup of water. Boil the water and at the time of boiling add the Myrrh and let it boil 3 more minutes. Rest another 3 minutes, strain and drink. **The essential oil should not be ingested or applied directly to the skin,** diluted in clay, vegetable oil or shampoo. **Contraindicated in pregnancy or lactation women.**

- Myrtle, (Mirto, en español)

"Myrtus communis", bush originating from middle East, used in the famous Patio de los Arrayanes in the Alhambra of Granada in Spain. It is grown as an ornamental plant in gardens and parks located in frost-free areas. In medicinal uses the infusion is used, also **the essential oil** that is extracted from the leaves **can be colored:** from light to yellow, orange or yellow-green. **In rare cases they can cause:** headaches and nausea. **Contraindicated in pregnancy or lactation women, under 6 years, in patients with gastritis, gastroduodenal ulcers, irritable bowel, Crohn's disease, ulcerative colitis, hepatic, epileptic, Parkinson's patients and any neurological disease, or in the process of ethylic dehabituation.**

Descriptions of plants letter N

- Naranjilla
- Narrow-leaf strap fern
- Nectarine
- Neroli oil
- Niaouli
- Noni, see Great morinda
- Nopal, see Indian fig opuntia
- Nutmeg
- Nymphaea, see Water Lily

- Naranjilla, (Naranjilla, en español)

"Solanum quitoense", plant and fruit typical of the Andes, grows spontaneously, the fruit is similar to a rounded yellow tomato, but its pulp is greenish normally and acid taste. Mature can be processed with its shell, increasing the level of benefits by taking advantage of the minerals and fiber contained in its external part. Normally it is consumed fresh or in juice, it has a positive influence on the organism just consumed, **it can ferment within a few hours** and be less healthy. **A lot of caution and prudence in persons suffering from gastrointestinal ulcers.**

- Narrow-leaf strap fern, (Calalagua, en español)

"Campyloneurum angustifolium", also know as Narrow strapfern, originating from Perú. Epiphyte plant, does not grow in the earth, is between crust and branches of other plants or in the middle of rocks. Fern species, stems and roots of the male fern are used in dressing or poultice or infusion. It exists in extract. **Contraindicated in persons with gastritis, duodenal ulcers and diabetes.**

- Nectarine, (Nectarina, en español)

"Prunus persica var. nucipersica", fruit of the tree originating from China, Afghanistan and Iran. It is a peach variety, the difference is in the skin, instead of velvety it is smooth and shiny, and tastes more acidic than it. **Contraindicated nectarine juice for diabetics.**

- Neroli oil, (Neroli, en español)

"Citrus Aurantinuma", is the essential oil distilled from the flowers of the bitter Orange "Citrus aurantium". Its name comes ...**Continue on next page**

... from the Princess of the Ursinos in Nerola, Italy (16th century). **As side effects it can cause:** malaise and headache in some persons. **Used too often it is addictive. To take orally, consult a doctor. Contraindicated in pregnancy and under 6 years.**

- Niaouli, (Niaoulí o Niaulí, en español)

"Melaleuca quinquenervia", also know as Broad-leaved paperbark, originating from Madagascar, of aromatic leaves that provide an essential oil of relaxing and healing virtues, with a sweet and fresh camphor smell. Widely used in hospitals in France as an antiseptic in obstetrics and gynecology. Its essential oil is used topically and internally as it is anti-infectious, both antibacterial and antiviral. **Contraindicated in pregnant women, under 6 years, persons with breast, ovarian or uterine cancer.**

- Nutmeg, (Nuez Moscada, en español)

"Myristica fragrans", originally from the Islands of spices (The Moluccas - Indonesia), the Arabs introduced it to Europe in the 11th century. **Its essential oil is poisonous,** it is used in cosmetics and topical use only, in foods it is used to aromatize. **It is recommended not to use more than 1 teaspoon per day in its use, it is potentially poisonous.** Avoid treatment **in long periods** for any remedy. **Contraindicated in pregnant women (abortive), or lactation, under 12 years and persons with liver diseases.**

Descriptions of plants letter O

- Olive
- Olm oak, see Evergreen oak
- Onion
- Orange
- Orange flame vine
- Oregano

- Olive, (Olivo, en español)

"Olea europaea", originating from the Mediterranean basin, since ancient times its wood and fruits (olives) are used. The infusions of crust and leaves are used for their healing properties. **In topical use only the crust.** The leaves in injectable or intravenously reduces blood pressure ...**Continue**

... and dilates the coronary arteries that surround the heart. **Possible side effects:** irritant to the gastric epithelium. **Contraindicated in pregnant women (unknown effects). Persons with gastric problems** ingest Olive oil alone in meals.

- Onion, (Cebolla, en español)

"Allium cepa", originating from Central Asia, **diabetics** are advised to **check their sugar levels,** since it can affect their level of consumption in abundance, it can affect them consumed in abundance. **You can also react with medications such as:** Aspirin, anticoagulants, anti platelets, and Lithium. **It is recommended to consult with the doctor in the group sensitive to all this.**

- Orange, (Naranjo dulce, en español)

"Citrus sinensis", it is believed to originating from China and Japan, nowadays it is cultivated in temperate countrie. There is a very curious variety, the orange of the sanguine type (its pulp and juice are reddish as blood). **The consumption of sweet oranges in juice or directly has many properties.** Its fresh leaves, **boiled for five minutes** have effective substances that help improve our health. **If the juice produces gas,** take out of time or ten minutes before meals. **Contraindicated in persons with very delicate stomachs.**

- Orange flame vine, (Combretum, en español)

"Combretum fruticosum", also know as Chameleon vine, it is a liana shrub native to America, from Mexico to Argentina, its properties and uses are similar to the African Combretum. **Use only under medical prescription. High doses cause:** vomiting, acidity, gastritis, and gastroduodenal ulcers. The leaves are used in different forms that are sold in specialized stores. **Contraindicated in pregnancy or lactation women, under 16 years and the elderly.**

- Oregano, (Orégano, en español)

"Origanum vulgare", originally from Asia Minor. An Arabic proverb says that oregano is good for everything, except for one thing, to cure death. It is very aromatic to grow in pots or in the garden. ...**Continue on next page**

... At recommended doses, oregano is a safe plant. **For therapeutic purposes,** the leaves are used in topical use or in infusions. Also as a condiment in salads, soups, fish. Also as a condiment in salads, soups, fish. **The essential oil** to be used in topical use **(ingested only under prescription),** dyes, fluid or dry extracts, suppositories, ointments, liniments and capsules are marketed. **The overdose can cause nervous alterations such as:** agitation, hyperesthesia, depression, dulling and drowsiness, or cardiac excitement due to the stimulating effects of its essential oil. **Contraindicated the essential oil in pregnancy or lactation women, under 12 years, anemic, patients with gastritis, gastroduodenal ulcers, irritable bowel syndrome, ulcerative colitis, Crohn's disease, hepatopathies, epilepsy, Parkinson's or other neurological diseases.**

Descriptions of plants letter P

- **Parsnip**
- **Passionflower**
- **Pea**
- **Peach**
- **Peanut**
- **Pennyroyal**
- **Peony or Paeony**
- **Perforate St John's-wort**
- **Perilla or Deulkkae**
- **Pineapple mint**
- **Pistachio**
- **Plectranthus, see Fragrant incense**
- **Pollen**
- **Polypodium fern**
- **Pomegranate**
- **Potato**
- **Primrose**
- **Pryckli pear**
- **Psoralea**
- **Purslane**

- Parsnip, (Chirivía, en español)
"Pastinaca sativa", originally from the warmest areas of Europe (although to develop completely needs frost and intermittent cold seasons). It is consumed in stews and soups, always after a cooking period. As a nutrient it is more complete than carrot, paler and different flavor. **...Continue**

... **There are no known contraindications,** it is **recommended to consult** with the doctor or specialist.

- Passionflower, (Pasiflora, en español)

"Passiflora caerulea", also know as Blue passionflower or Maypop, it is native to the south of the USA, Central America, Brazil and Peru. Beautiful and aromatic flower. The fruit is a berry ovoid, fleshy, acid taste, orange and black seeds. Administered orally, it is well tolerated, it does not cause side effects. **In excess it can produce:** dizziness, confusion and irregular coordination. It is taken in infusion, or in juice, there are dry and fluid extracts, tincture. **Extreme caution when combined with:** Nembutal, Seconal, Lorazepam, Luminal, etc. **It can produce extreme drowsiness**, and make normal life difficult, as well as reduce the conditions for driving or operating machinery. **Contraindicated in pregnancy (some of their substances could contract the uterus), and lactation women.**

- Pea, (Guisante, en español)

"Pisum sativum", the origin of the green pea is related to the Middle East and Central Asia, where it is cultivated since the 8th century BC, advanced the 2th century BC, it would spread for Europe. It is one of the **recommended foods for those who can not consume dairy products.** Its consumption is recommended in all ages. **To avoid gas problems,** consume in the form of puree. **There are no known contraindications,** it is **recommended to consult** with the doctor or specialist.

- Peach, (Melocotón, en español)

"Prunus pérsica", in China it was cultivated 2,000 years before it was known by the ancient Greeks and Romans, it was introduced in Europe at the beginning of the Christian era. **It is not advisable to consume frequently under 6 years,** it can cause diarrhea and stomach aches. **Neither do persons with thyroid disease.**

- Peanut, (Cacahuete, en español)

"Arachis hypogaea", originating from the Andean region of Peru, there are archaeological records of its consumption 8,000 years ago. In spite of its bad reputation it is very beneficial for health and ...**Continue on next page**

... for multiple ailments, be it toasted, oil or cream. **Contraindicated in renal patients or patients with gallbladder problems (due to its oxalate content).**

- Pennyroyal or Pennyrile, (Poleo o Menta poleo, en español)
"Mentha pulegium", native to the Mediterranean basin, grows in wet places, the infusions are very popular, for the relaxing effect they generate. **It can be toxic when the allowed doses are exceeded.** Combined with other medicines or plants, it can enhance its effects, **consult with the doctor, in case of being medicated against some ailment. The** way to consume is in infusions, **the habitual use can produce:** hypoglycemia, it can decrease the levels of iron in the blood, because it inhibits its absorption. **Caution with excess infusions ingested, as a side effect may cause:** diarrhea, dizziness, mental confusion, sore throat, difficulty swallowing, muscle weakness, headache, ringing in the ears, convulsions, thirst, sweat excessive, weak pulse and paralysis of the muscles of respiration, **in excess death by coma. In topical use the infusion or the essential oil can:** affect the skin in the form of dermatitis, itching, restlessness, malaise, itching in the eyes, etc. **Contraindicated in pregnant (abortive), or lactation women.**

- Peony or Paeony, (Peonia, en español)
"Paeoniaceae", original from Europe, of great ornamental value, the most appreciated is dark red, although this species has white or slightly violet flowers. The fruit is of capsular form that encloses a good amount of black seeds. **Plant with a certain toxicity, in high doses can become deadly.** For therapeutic uses, flowers, seeds and roots are used. The most used form is in infusion that is prepared with a teaspoon of coffee from the parts we want by cup of water, boil 15 minutes, strain and drink about 3 cups a day. **Never use as a laxative.** Tincture, fluid extract and cicatrizant gel are also found. All forms must be **used in a discontinuous manner. Contraindicated ingested in pregnant women (abortive), or lactation, in under 6 years.**

- Perforate St John's-wort or Hypericum, (Hipérico, en español)
"Hypericum perforatum", very common in Europe where it originates. It grows on fresh slopes, uncultivated land and meadows not excessively humid. The whole plant or flowers are used, mainly the floral tops of the upper part of the stem. It is sold as whole fresh or dry herb for infusions and decoctions, powder or grajeas, cryogenic powder, tonics, oil, ointments and dermatological creams, extracts, hard capsules and soft, blisters. **Its results are widely contrasted** in mild and moderate depressions, **its effects are observed at two or three weeks of treatment.** This plant can replace drugs of chemical origin **with mixtures for depression with other** pathologies added. **As side effects, some persons can cause:** gastrointestinal discomfort, dry mouth, nervousness and hives, on the other hand, persons of skin or clear eyes have to avoid the sun while they take it. **Contraindicated prolonged use in pregnancy or lactation women, and with antidepressant medications.**

- Perilla or Deulkkae, (Perilla o Shiso, en español)
native to South Asia, China, India, Japan, Laos, Thailand, Vietnam. It belongs to **the family of plants such as Mints and Peppermints. It uses** the leaves and the whole plant. The habitual consumption is in infusion with ¼ cup with dried powdered leaves, to cover with boiling water and let boil for 10 to 15 minutes. Shiso / Deulkkae oil is also used for specific ailments. **Contraindicated in cancer patients, in pregnancy or lactation women, under 12 years, do not consume in medication with anti-inflammatories or against cholesterol.**

- Pineapple mint, (Mentastro, en español)
"Mentha suaveolens", of European origin, rare in northern Europe, its properties are very similar to mints, it grows in areas near wetlands between reeds and brambles. **It is somewhat toxic.** The form of use is in infusion. **Contraindicated in pregnancy or lactation women, and under 6 years.**

- Pistachio, (Pistacho, en español)

"Pistacia vera", fruit of the tree of the same name, originating in western Asia from mountainous regions of Greece to Pakistan, the highest quality are those of Iran. Bright green color, with a high caloric content, and with interesting medicinal properties. **Contraindicated in case of chronic renal failure.**

- Pollen, (Polen, en español)

Exception of the book, it is included in the coming from the plants serving in its multiplication, and by the benefits attributed from the antiquity, has led to its recognition as a product of high nutritional value. Endowed with prophylactic revitalizing and therapeutic properties. It contains all the essentia elements for life, and the restoration and maintenance of the health of the body. **The allergics should not consume pollen.** Considered a food superior to any vegetable or artificial vitamin. **There are no known contraindications,** it is **recommended to consult** with the doctor or specialist

- Polypodium fern, (Helecho polipodio, en español)

"Polypodium vulgare", also know as Polypody fern, it develops naturally in almost all of Europe. The most common growth zone are walls, rock edges, tree trunks and similar sites. If it is collected for medicinal purposes, remove the green parts and dry in sunlight (dry storage can be kept for up to 12 months). The taste of the root is sweet (it contains sucrose), it can be used without any inconvenience as a natural sweetener. The very effective powder, should take about 3 gr. a day (distributed in different meals). Decoction is the most widespread way to use. Any dosage with alcohol content should **not be used by under 6 years** or persons **with ethyl problems. There are no known contraindications,** it is **recommended to consult** with the doctor or specialist.

- Pomegranate, (Granado / Granada, en español)

"Punica granatum", originating from Persia (Iran), has been cultivated for more than 5,000 years in western Asia. Its fruit enters the Hebrew, Christian and Masonic symbology. Fruit with a high ...**Continue**

... antioxidant power, rich in vitamins and multiple medicinal benefits. Seeds, flowers, crust, etc. are used, and in many cases its juice is recommended to obtain its properties more easily. Whatever the form, it should be taken at least three months to assess its effects. **May cause:** nausea, vomiting, abdominal pain and diarrhea by excessive intake of seeds or juice, which rarely persist, disappear in a couple of hours. **Avoid eating oily foods** with it. **Do not consume allergy sufferers. Persons with constipation should not abuse the juice.**

- Potato, (Patata, en español)

"Solanum tuberosum", originating from Andes, formerly it was believed that it was not edible, even poisonous. Today it is one of the most universal and cheap foods of which there are many varieties. It has a bad reputation, due to ignorance, when many people consider one of the first members to leave their diet when it is a loaded tuber of nutrients and a wide variety of vitamins, minerals and phytochemicals that help prevent disease and benefit our health. **Caution, with the solanine, green substance that is just under the skin,** eat the raw potato or with skin (in abundance) it can be a danger to our health, being a **natural pesticide.** It is advisable **to remove the skin perfectly and consume the potatoes immediately,** the concentrations of solanine increase the older the potato is. **It is recommended to cook the potato without skin to prevent this alkaloid can affect us.**

- Primrose, (Primavera, en español)

"Primula vulgaris", original from the West and South of Europe. Of plants that before bloom and if the winter is not very cold you can find the first flowers (very aromatic) in mid-January. The most common and abundant **"Primula veris" is used** in the Iberian Peninsula (protected in some places, **better to refrain from collecting. Cultivated and ornamental varieties are not adequate,** cause irritation. As therapeutic use the flowers and the root (mainly), contains substances related with Acetyl Salicylic Acid or Aspirin. **For the remedies is used the root in dry form, and the flowers when they have (never start the whole plant).** ...Continue on nex page

... It exists in specialty stores, creams and spring ointments. **There are no known contraindications,** it is **recommended to consult** with the doctor or specialist.

- Pryckli pear, (Higo chumbo o Tuna, en español)

"Opuntia ficus-indica", also know as Indian fig opuntia or Barbary fig, originating from Mexico, fruit quite unknown in many countries, difficult to collect and peel. It is used in the preparation of different beauty products such as shampoo, creams and gels for their enormous medicinal qualities. **Caution persons with urinary tract infections. Contraindicated in persons with a reduced fluid intake, serious cardiac or renal pathologies.**

- Psoralea, (Psoralea o Culen, en español)

"Psoralea glandulosa" or "Otholobium glandulosum", also know as Otholobium, originating from Argentina, Peru, Chile and Uruguay, of strong, vertical stems and some villi. The leaves are very aromatic, and the tips transparent. It can be found in dry meadows, stony slopes, abandoned lands, roadsides in crops. **There are no known contraindications,** it is **recommended to consult** with the doctor or specialist.

- Pumpkin, (Calabaza, en español)

"Cucurbita máxima", originating from Mexico and Texas, has been cultivating for more than 4,000 years. With the exception of its roots, for therapeutic purposes **it is used in internal or topical use:** leaves, flower, fruit (pumpkin) and its seeds (pumpkin seeds). The seed does not irritate or are toxic, it can be consumed without any fear. The flower, large and similar to the bells, but yellow orange, can be coated in flour. Consuming raw flower in salads, soups or steamed, they take better advantage of their properties. There are preparations with pumpkin seeds. Its richness in vitamin E makes them important for the pituitary (development gland) and reproduction. **Avoid excess pumpkin seeds, persons who suffer:** ulcerative colitis, gastric ulcers or hiatus hernias (causes burning, heartburn), with gastritis (worsens symptoms). **Contraindicated with anticoagulant medication (produces opposite effect).**

- Purslane or Verdolaga, (Verdolaga, en español)

"Portulaca oleracea", originating from Mediterranean basin and zones of Europe of warm climate. Known since antiquity for its therapeutic properties, but ignorance makes you despise things of enormous value and in this case the Purslane is considered by many as a weed. However, it contains Omega 3, and make it one of the vegetables richest in these essential fatty acids. Of leaves in the form of tears, dark Green color, stem between reddish and violet, grows wild and even in gardens. It can be consumed fresh in salads or other raw presentations. Cooked sautéed or steamed. If you opt for your juice, it is recommended to drink a maximum of 100 gr. of fresh plant or 1 to 3 tablespoons that can be mixed with water or honey (over 1 year). In the infusions to ingest the fresh or dry plant is used, it is cooked for a few seconds so that the oxalic acid do not go into the water, being the usual form of consumption. Also the tea of its seeds. It exists in the market in **alcohol tincture not suitable for children or persons in the process of dehabituation** ethylic. **There are no known contraindications,** it is **recommended to consult** with the doctor or specialist.

Descriptions of plants letter Q

- Quince
- Quinine

- Quince, (Membrillo, en español)

"Cydonia oblonga", originating from Iran and Turkey, but cultivated in large areas of the planet. The pulp and the seeds of the fruit are that possess medicinal qualities. It can be consumed raw, cooked, roasted, depending on the taste or the needs of use. **There are no known contraindications,** it is **recommended to consult** with the doctor or specialist.

- Quinine, (Quina, en español)

"Cinchona officinalis", tree originating from Peruvian Amazon. Due to its widespread use and commercial exploitation, it is now in danger of extinction worldwide. The crust of the branches, the trunk dried and the root have active principles. The infusion is...Continue on next page

... prepared with 10 gr. of crust per liter of boiling water. It is advised to take 2 cups a day. It is obtained in powder, liquid extract, tincture, syrup. Quinine wine is curative (**in adults** only 1 glass a day is enough to obtain good results). **With moderation does not generate contraindications, in very high doses can produce:** vomiting, nausea, headache and ear problems.

Descriptions of plants letter R

- Red pepper
- Reishi mushroom
- Rice
- Rockrose, see Cistus

- Rose
- Rose hip / hep / haw
- Rosemary,
- Rue

- Red pepper, (Pimiento rojo, en español)

"Capsicum annuum", originating from America, being known in Europe by the Spanish in the 16th century, is the most mature of peppers, can be eaten raw, boiled or roasted. **Abstain patients with gastritis, gastroduodenal ulcers.**

- Reishi mushroom, (Reishi, en español)

"Ganoderma lucidum", also know as Lingzhi mushroom, it grows mainly on the decaying trunks of the wild plum, sometimes on the oak. It is mentioned in the oldest document of the Chinese Pharmacopoeia in 56 B.C. and it is believed that Asians knew Reishi centuries and even millennia before. It is very rare in nature, only grows in the mountains, and deep forests. Today it is cultivated in an artificial environment in China, Asia and North America. **Use on prescription and in personalized treatment by a trained professional.** It is consumed in the form of tablets, capsules, and in solid or liquid extract. **As side effects can cause:** dry mouth, throat and nasal passages, itching, nosebleed and diarrhea. **Contraindicated in persons with hypotension, Thrombocytopenia, before and after surgery or delivery.**

- Rice, (Arroz, en español)

"Oryza sativa", it is the most consumed cereal in the world, next to corn. Asia has been consuming it for more than 5,000 years. There are approximately 170 species of arable rice. China is the country that most cultivates and consumes it. Normally the rice consumed is the so-called "polished", from which the starch has been extracted of its outer layers (the most nutritious). But it is the most effective for diarrhea. If consumed in large quantities, it causes scurvy. Due to its deficiency in lysine, it is recommended to cook with vegetables, fresh vegetables or accompanied by abundant raw salad. The best is brown rice, but its appearance repels some persons. Its gluten-free protein is **ideal for coeliacs.** There is a **rice syrup** as a sweetener. **Consult with the doctor or specialist persons suffering from Crohn's disease, ulcerative colitis.**

- Rose, (Rosal, en español)

"Rosa Gallica", also know as Gallic rose, originally from Central Europe and West Asia. The flowers are gathered in groups of one to four, with their very wide color, there are 30,000 varieties, from the white (rare) to pink or dark purple, being what petals the employees to elaborate medicinal remedies. Here the most common one is described for therapeutic purposes, that where the rose petals can be used to complement other preparations giving a pleasant flavor to the infusions. The infusion is the usual way, is prepared with a teaspoon of dried petals per cup **(should not boil).** It is marketed products made with roses, rose water, ointments, essential oil. **During pregnant women** (only under facultative prescription). **Contraindicated during lactating mothers, under 6 years, and persons with gastric ulcer.**

- Rose hip / hep / haw, (Escaramujo, en español)

"Rosa micrantha", it is the wild rose, an excellent antidiarreic and with many beneficial properties for the skin. It usually flowers in spring, and its fruits mature in late summer and autumn. Fruits, leaves, petals and even roots are used. **Your abuse can cause constipation because it is high in tannins.** It is taken in infusions with other herbs for each specific case of the skin. **Consuming in moderation ...Continue on next page**

... pregnancy or lactation women, it could **lead to constipation. Alcohol-based tinctures are contraindicated for under 6 years or persons in the process of alcohol cessation.**

- **Rosemary,** (Romero, en español)
"Rosmarinus officinalis", native of the Mediterranean basin, for medicinal purposes the flowering tops are used. It is commercialized in dry form, tinctures fluid extracts and dry extracts, there is also essential oil. **Contraindicated essential oil, ingested, in pregnancy or lactation women, under 6 years, patients with gastritis, gastroduodenal ulcers, irritable bowel syndrome, ulcerative colitis, Crohn's disease, liver disease, epilepsy, Parkinson's or other neurological diseases. In topical use in children under 6 years, persons with respiratory allergies or known hypersensitivity to essential oils, or with problems of obstruction of the bile ducts. Contraindicated tincture with alcohol content in under 12 years, or persons in the process of alcoholic dependence).**

- **Rue,** (Ruda, en español)
"Ruta graveolens", also know as Herb of grace, originally from southern Europe, it is usually used as a condiment, **used with caution** is a plant with many medicinal properties. It is used therapeutically in: capsules, tincture and infusion. The dose is **1 gr. maximum, under prescription and medical surveillance, due to its high toxicity, it is not advisable to use it long.** Very useful against insects, it is used in insecticide products such as vaporizers, wands, etc. It can help to ward off and fight pests. **The essential oil is quite toxic, it is not recommended to apply on the skin,** it can cause redness, and ailments such as: dermatitis, spots or blisters (watch their use). **It is less toxic to consume the dry leaves due to the volatility of the essential oil. Contraindicated in pregnant women (abortive), or lactation, under 12 years persons with renal problems, hepatic insomnia, gastric, duodenal ulcers, colitis, their effects can even damage the respiratory system, causing cardiorespiratory stops and death.**

Descriptions of plants letter S

- Seville orange, see Bitter orange
- Single-seeded hawthorn, see Common hawthorn
- Sundrops, see Evening primrose
- Sweet flag, see
- Calamus
- Sweet granadilla, see Grenadia
- Stavesacre, see Lice-Bane
- Sage
- Salep drink
- Small-leaved lime
- Stevia
- Saturn peaches
- Seneca snakeroot
- Siberian ginseng
- Silver wattle
- Soursop
- Southern magnolia
- Spearmint
- Spirulina
- Strawberry plant/
- Strawberries
- Sugarcane or Sugar cane
- Sumatra benzoin tree
- Sumbal
- Summer savory
- Sunflower
- Sweetscented bedstraw

- Sage, (Salvia, en español)

"Salvia officinalis", also know as Garden sage, originating from Mediterranean basin, the most usual form is the infusion, **never more than three infusions a day. Do not exceed the recommended dose:** it can be neurotoxic and cause seizures. **Contraindicated in pregnant women (abortive), or lactation, under 6 years, persons with breast cancer and other estrogen-dependent tumors, patients with neurovegetative instability, or renal failure.**

- Salep drink, (Salep, en español)

"Anacamptis papilionácea – fam. Orchis", also know as Butterfly orchid drink, originating from Mediterranean basin. In Turkey these orchids are used to make a very energetic traditional drink that strengthens health, elevating the organic defenses for when the cold climates of winter begin. This drink is called "Salep", the starch or aromatic flour of the tubers, in particular of the wild species, "Satirión orchis" and "Ophrys holosericea". Its prepare with 4 cups of milk, 1 cup of sugar, 1 tablespoon of Salep, mix the sweetener with the Salep in a pot. Add cold milk and mix. **Instead of sugar (without any nutritional value), any sweetener can be used (see in Sweeteners).** Mix while boiling, on fire slow for 2-3 minutes, serve hot spraying with a little Cinnamon, you can add a little Starch. Salep is sold prepared, for heat and consume. **There are no known contraindications, it is recommended to consult** with the doctor or specialist.

- Summer savory, (Ajedrea o Hisopillo, en español)

"Satureja hortensis", plant native to Eurasia, stems, leaves and dried flowers are used. Very used in the Bulgarian and Romanian cuisine especially for its typical dish, the "Sarmale". **The essence** of this plant can be **very reactive** in some persons and there is a **slight risk of causing allergies. Special care in children. Contraindicated in pregnancy or lactation women.**

- Saturn peaches, (Paraguaya, en español)

"Prunus persica var. Platycarpa", originating from **Persia (Irán) o China,** the Paraguayan tree is obtained by means of mutations of the peach tree. The fruit is a variety of peach with similar nutritional characteristics. **There are no known contraindications,** it is **recommended to consult** with the doctor or specialist.

- Seneca snakeroot, (Polygala senega, en español)

"Polygala senega", native of North America, is distributed by the south of Canada, center and east of the USA. **Always use under medical prescription.** It is marketed in tinctures, syrups, dry extracts and fluids. The infusion is made with 3 tablespoons per liter, boil 2 minutes. Rest for 10 minutes, strain and drink 3 or 4 cups a day. ...**Continue**

... Overdose can cause: gastrointestinal irritation. **Contraindicated in patients with gastroduodenal ulcer, ulcerative colitis, in dosage with alcohol content in under 2 years, and persons in the process of alcohol ceasstion.**

- Siberian ginseng, (Eleuterococo, en español)

"Eleutherococcus senticosus", belongs to the Ginseng family, comes from the steppes of Siberia. Used by athletes **can give positive in doping.** Its benefits and properties are so important and outstanding that even after interrupting the treatment the reinforcement of the resistance of the organism will be constant and sustained over time. **Before use consult your doctor if you have suffered or suffer:** acute myocardial infarction, cardiac arrhythmias, severe arterial hypertension, coronary heart disease, acute infections, fever.

- Silver wattle, (Mimosa, en español)

"Acacia dealbata", also know as Mimosa, of Australian origin, of flowers grouped with golden yellow colors and very aromatic. Flowers and buds are used, in order to realize essential oil, non-toxic, do not act as skin irritant. It is used orally from 2 to 3 drops per day. In topical use 1 drop locally. **There are no known contraindications,** it is **recommended to consult** with the doctor or specialist.

- Small-leaved lime, (Tila alpina, en español)

"Tilia cordata", originating from Europe, from Spain to the mountns and mountains of Russia and Turkey. Tree of the genus "Tilia", narrow leaf. It is easily distinguished from "Tilia platyphyllos", of broadleaf. The flowers, leaves and crust are used as a therapeutic remedy. **The best way to consume is the infusion,** up to two cups a day, ideal before bedtime, or to spend an afternoon or a relaxed day, also before an examitation, an interview. To prepare it is recommended once the water is boiled, in a cup put no more than 1.5 grams and rest. **Use only for specific cases**, not as a routine drink. **Contains tannins,** excessive consumption **over time can diminish its positive relaxing effects. Contraindicated in persons suffering from hypotension.**

- Soursop, (Graviola, en español)

"Annona muricata", originating from México, Caribbean, Central and South America. The whole plant, leaves, fruits (similar to the Cherimoya), flowers, stems, roots and crust are used. **Consume the fruit in moderation,** start with a minimum dose and increase each day or week. The part with more "power" is the leaves in infusion. **In high doses it can alter the intestinal flora (constipation or diarrhoea). Contraindicated in pregnancy women and persons with heart or blood problems.**

- Southern magnolia, (Magnolia, en español)

"Magnolia grandiflora", also know as Bull bay, tree originating in China, there are records of several thousand years. For natural remedies, crust and flowers are used mainly. **Use extracts already prepared,** which, together with the supplements included, are extremely powerful. In large doses cause: vertigo, dizziness and headaches. **The crust can cause:** respiratory paralysis in animals and in under 12 years. **Contraindicated in pregnancy, under 12 years, and persons with liver, spleen or stomach failure.**

- Spearmint, (Hierbabuena, en español)

"Mentha spicata", originating from Middle East and Asia. For **under 6 years** **and in pregnant women** it can cause **anemia** by inhibiting the absorption of iron. **In excess it can cause liver damage.** The usual way to swallow is the infusion. **A lot of caution:** diabetics, persons taking antacids, cyclosporine, with hiatus hernia, GERD or gastroesophageal reflux disease, those medicated for the liver or hypertension.

- Spirulina, (Espirulina, en español)

"Arthrospira máxima" and "Arthrospira platensis", are two components of this species of algae considered a superfood against weight loss. They are not harmful supplements. **It can produce side effects such as:** thirst, constipation, some fever, slight dizziness, stomach pain, headache, itching or rash on the skin. **Use under medical supervision during pregnancy or lactation women and persons with hyperthyroidism or hypothyroidism because of its iodine content.**

- **Stevia,** (Stevia, en español)

"Stevia rebaudiana", also know as Sugarleaf, originating from South America, it can still be found in wild way, it is currently cultivated for consumption. It is a powerful sweetener, **has hardly any calories or carbohydrates** (1 gr. of Stevia has 1 calorie and 1 gr. of carbohydrates), **no fat or cholesterol.** The leaves contain a variety of nutrients, such as **proteins, fiber, carbohydrates, vitamins A and C, and minerals such as sodium, magnesium, iron, phosphorus, calcium, potassium, and zinc,** in processed form are not appreciated. There is a white powder like sugar being 200 to 300 times sweeter than it and leaves between 15 and 20 times. **You can use the fresh plant,** small pieces of a leaf, according to the sweetness to be desired. To be used several times in different preparations such as biscuits, cakes or infusions, Boil leaves in a liter of water and keep the obtained liquid in a cool place. **They exist:** sachets (to mix with other tisanes), dry leaves, essence, pills, liquid extract and powder. **It can cause allergic reactions in persons sensitive to:** plants of the families of Chrysanthemum and Daisy. **Side effects include:** nausea, abdominal distension and gas. At very high levels it can affect the hypotensive. **Contraindicated in pregnant and lactating women.**

- Strawberry plant/Strawberries, (Fresal / Fresa, en español)

"Fragaria", originating from Eurasia, plant used as food and medicine since ancient times. The fruits are rich in vitamin C, they also have A and B, in addition to mineral salts and many other substances. The leaves for medicinal use are collected in summer when the plant is in flower. The roots are harvested in the spring or autumn. **Consume with moderation persons in diarrheal processes, allergic to aspirin, with renal lithiasis by oxalates, with anticoagulant medication or problems to absorb iron.**

- Sumbal, (Sumbul, en español)

"Férula sumbul", also know as Muskroot, herbaceous native to southern Russia, Turkestan and northern India, the stem exudes a milky sap when broken. It was first brought from Russia in 1535 as a substitute for Musk, in 1867 it was introduced into the British Pharmacopoeia. Stem leaves progressively decrease in size to the top where they are mere bracts. The whole plant has an intense smell of musk. ...**Continue on next page**

... For medicinal uses their roots and rhizomes are used, **follow the indications of a specialist.** It is sold in powders, fluid and dry extracts. **Excessive doses can cause narcotic effects, confusion, tingling and nasal discharge.**

- Sugarcane or Sugar cane, (Caña de azúcar, en español)

"Saccharum officinarum", sugarcane integral sugar is one of the richest sweeteners in vitamins and minerals. **Consider that the excess of this sugar is detrimental to the dental health.** It varies **the conditions when used in juice, it should be consumed** as soon as it is extracted, it tends to oxidize in 15 minutes. The sugar is obtained by evaporating the juice of the cane by heating or lyophilization, **of all the types of sugar is the healthiest by containing some minerals and vitamins when the artisan process of elaboration is respected.** The true whole cane sugar **is not brown,** has a **slightly toasted color and cakes easily** to contact with moisture. There is cane molasses. **Contraindicated for diabetics and persons intolerant of glucose.**

- Sumatra benzoin tree, (Benjuí, en español)

"Styrax benzoin", tree of the forests of Laos, Vietnam, Malaysia, Indonesia. Its resin is mainly used internally, or in ointments, soaps, tinctures, essential oil. **The resin can be drunk according to specialist indications.** Inhalation is another way to take advantage of your medicinal benefits. **Contraindicated in pregnancy or lactation women, under 12 years, persons with chronic and allergic illnesses.**

- Sunflower, (Girasol, en español)

"Helianthus annuus", originating from Tibetan mountains, grows wild and its cultivation has expanded to many regions of the world. Others place it from the center and north of America. Its cultivation dates back to the year 1000 BC, but there are data indicating that the sunflower was domesticated in Mexico at least 2,600 BC. The seeds they have a high calorie content. **In large quantities, its consumption is not recommended for persons who are markedly overweight.**

- Sweetscented bedstraw, (Aspérula, en español)

"Galium odoratum", Eurasian plant, very effective for various ailments. **As a somnifera only should be used by seniors.** The whole plant is used, except for the root, the infusion and liquefaction are the usual ways to alleviate the discomfort. **The overdose produces headaches.**

Descriptions of plants letter T

- Tamarillo
- Tamarind
- Tansy
- Trarragon, see Estragon
- Tea of Aragon
- Thyme
- Tila tree
- Tequila agave, see Blue agave
- Tick-trefoil or Tick clover
- Turk's cap Lily, see Martagon lily
- Turmeric

- Tamarillo, (Tomate de árbol, en español)

"Solanum betaceum", fruit also know as Tree tomato, originating from Andes and little known, it is found wild or cultivated throughout South America. It is medium-sized, smooth, bright and brick color or red when ripe and acid-sweet taste. It is consumed as fresh fruit, although due to the excess acidity, in many cases, mix the juice with water or milk. Also the juice as a soda directly, to do this boil 10 minutes the tomatoes with shell, without pedicle, let cool, remove the peel manually. Blend 3 tomatoes, and depending on taste you can add carrots, pineapple, blackberry, water, a little milk and sweeten to taste. Directly or raw, slice the fruit in small pieces and add lemon to taste. It is used as raw material in the industry for the preparation of juices, compotes, sweet preserves, jellies, gelatine, jams and frozen concentrates. You can find pre-prepared bags of concentrates in some Spanish-speaking American products stores. **Contraindicated in persons with skin allergies, low blood pressure (hypotensive), and suffer from hives.**

- **Tamarind,** (Tamarindo, en español)

"Tamarindus indica", originating from Africa, but cultivated with great success in part of tropical Asia and Ibero - America. **Fruits brown or dark coffee that look like small sacks. The pulp is an excellent condiment** to prepare dressings and sauces. Africans often mix pulp with rice. **The pulp is used, leaves and crust in medicinal applications**. It is very useful in places where it is very hot to fight dehydrations. **Contraindicated in pregnancy or lactation women and eat, if you take aspirin, for the possible increase in bleeding.**

- **Tansy,** (Tanaceto, en español)

"Tanacetum vulgare", originating from Southeast Europe and Asia Minor, bush of aromatic leaves, divided and hairy dark green, flowers of white petals and the yellow central button. In the Middle Ages until the 17th century, in England and northern Spain its use was widespread as a remedy for all kinds of diseases. The leaves and flowers are used in infusion, there are tinctures and essential oil. **Contraindicated in pregnancy women (abortive), or lactation, in persons with problems of blood clotting or low platelets.**

- **Tea of Aragon,** (Té de roca, en español)

"Jasonia glutinosa" or "Chiliadenus glutinosus", also know as Rock tea, originating from Western Mediterranean countries, from Provence to Morocco, it grows between the stones, forming a small bush of 30 cm, of small yellow flowers at the end of the stem, although called tea, **it does not contain theine, and in large doses produces vomiting.** Essential oil is sold. The usual way is in infusions, of strong smell and bitter flavor, better sweeten to taste, see Sweeteners. Drink up to two cups a day. **Contraindicated in pregnancy women (abortive), or lactation.**

- **Thyme,** (Tomillo, en español)

"Thymus vulgaris", originating from Mediterranean basin and Asia, there are about 1,500 species, a very aromatic shrub of woody stems, with small pale pink or white flowers grouped in very dense clusters. The plant is recognized quickly because it gives off a strong aroma. ...**Continue**

... Due to its bactericidal properties it was used in antiquity to embalm mummies. There is an essential oil, **before using it is recommended consult with the doctor or specialist.** The usual form is the infusion, ingested or in topical use as rinses, mouthwashes, **without sweetening.** Also as a condiment in stews, **little,** the taste is very intense. **There are no known contraindications,** it is **recommended to consult** with the doctor or specialist.

- Tick-trefoil or Tick clover, (Desmodium, en español)

"Desmodium adscendens", originally from Sierra Leone and north of Liberia. **The most important plant for liver problems.** It is widely used in infusions, also in capsules and extracts with plants such as Milk Thistle or Blessed milkthistle, Artichoke, Dandelion, Boldo, etc. In phytotherapy, stems and leaves are used. **In very high doses can cause nausea and diarrhea,** these effects are passed by reducing the dose. Its toxicity level is not significant, it is **recommended to consult** with the **doctor or specialist.**

- Tila tree, (Tila, en español)

"Tilia platyphyllos", also know as Large-leaved lime, it is obtained from the broad-leaved tree and deciduous, grows spontaneously in the forests of Europe, Asia and North America, can also be found in streets and urban parks in cities around the world. The healing properties of the Tila are known since antiquity, its flowers are used, very aromatic and in cluster form. There are totally natural pills to facilitate your intake and have more control of the treatment. **It is advisable to avoid** its consumption **or to consult with the doctor:** during **pregnancy, in case of coronary disease or chronic digestive problems.**

- Turmeric, (Cúrcuma, en español)

"Curcuma longa", originating from southwest of India, used since the 7th century BC. Yellow or mustard and specific flavor that gives another taste to the meals. It is consumed by sprinkling, rinsing, as a dye, or for drinking (unpleasant taste, better to mask), to cauterize small wounds. **Contraindicated in pregnancy or lactation women, patients with gallbladder problems, with gastroesophageal reflux disease(GERD), newly operated (delays coagulation and cause additional bleeding).**

Descriptions of plants letter V

- Vachellia aroma
- Valerian
- Vanilla
- Verdolaga, see Purslane
- Vervain
- Vetiver
- Viper's bugloss
- Virginia water horehound
- Vitex

- Vachellia aroma or Aromita, (Aromita o Espinillo, en español)
"Acacia aroma", Uruguayan tree of the Acacia family grows profusely leaving the soil unusable for agriculture. The crust, leaves and seeds have healing properties diluting 20 gr. in 1 liter of boiling water serves as an infusion for external use and ingested. **Use under medical supervision, pregnancy or lactation women, under 12 years, and persons with chronic diseases.**

- Valerian, (Valeriana, en español)
"Valeriana officinalis", originating from Europe, one of the most used medicinal herbs along with the Tila and Passionflower for almost the same remedies. Plant with several active ingredients used for pharmaceutical purposes, is used mainly the root and sometimes the flowers. **Do not take for a period greater than 10-12 days**. It can be combined with other plants of similar properties such as Melissa/Lemon balm, Passionflower **(under 12 years not recommended),** Chamomile, etc. Commercialized in dry leaves, prepared in sachets, pills, in addition to being one of the primary ingredients for the preparation of essential oils. **Contraindicated in pregnancy or lactation women, under 6 years, in persons taking sedative medications or those that affect the central nervous system.** Incompatible with alcohol, and in drivers **(causes drowsiness).**

- Vanilla, (Vainilla, en español)

"Vanilla planifolia", is one of the 110 existing "Vanilla" species, orchid creeper originatin from Mexico, there are more than 30 varieties, here the most used as a flavoring is described, grown in tropical areas of America, mainly. It consumes the fruit that comes out of a flower that barely lasts open for a couple of days, with an unmistakable and exquisite smell, forming a blackish pod where it keeps the seeds. Used by the Aztecs as a healing remedy, even Hernán Cortés came to know it. From the 17th century it expanded through French cuisine. In synergy with chocolate increases endorphins enhancing their properties. The usual for curative remedies is infusion, also mixed with other foods. The generalized commercializationis in branch, powder, tincture and essential oil. **Contraindicated ingest the essential oil in pregnancy or lactation women, under 12 years, patients with gastroduodenal ulcers, colitis, liver and kidney disease.**

- Vervain, (Verbena, en español)

"Verbena officinalis", It grows in Southeast Europe, Asia, Africa and America, the harvest is made during the summer months when they open their flowers (dry in the shade). In the curative remedies the buds of the flowers and the leaves of the plant are used in infusion. **Contraindicated in pregnant women (abortive), or lactation, and on under 12 years.**

- Vetiver, (Vetiver, en español)

"Chrysopogon zizanioides", originally from India, it is used for the construction of houses or huts for its antiseptic, aromatic and mosquito repellent value, even when it is dry. Apart from its curative or industrial properties in perfumery, soaps and cosmetics. It is mainly used the extract of its essential oil that is obtained from the roots. Use as directed by the preparations or specialist. **Contraindicated in pregnancy or lactation women.**

- Viper's bugloss or Blueweed, (Viborera, en español)

"Echium vulgare", originally from Europe and Asia minor, it is easy to recognize because of its distinctive exterior appearance, **resembling** Borage and **Bugloss (caution).** It can be found ...**Continue on next page**

... especially on roadsides, river banks. For the healing remedies, the leaves and stems are infused, you can prepare them with a handful of leaves per cup of water, boil, strain and drink up to 4 cups a day. The same infusion can be used in topical use in washing or poultice, without sweetening. **Prolonged use may be toxic to the liver.** It can also be consumed fresh like any other vegetable. **Contraindicated in pregnant women (abortive), or lactation, and on under 6 years.**

- Virginia water horehound, (Menta de lobo, en español)

"Lycopus virginicus" or "Lycopus europaeus", they are two similar varieties in properties, also know as European bugleweed or Gypsywort, originating from North America del Norte (Virginia) and Europe, it has been used since time immemorial, a species with perennial flowers that is commonly used for medicinal purposes. Each spring the plant blooms with bright purple flowers. **Do not ingest in medication related to hormones, chemotherapy, sedatives.**

- Vitex or Chaste tree, (Sauzgatillo, en español)

"Vitex agnus-castus", originally from southern Europe and central Asia, it grows in temperate climates on the banks of currents or humid places, small flowers, tubular, lilac, aromatic, fleshy fruits between reds and blacks. Used in antiquity as **a remedy for women,** the properties are numerous for them in particular, the infusion is made by pouring a spoonful of slightly crushed berries (better fresh) in a boiling cup. Rest for 10 minutes, strain and drink warm. **It can rarely provoke:** gastrointestinal discomfort and mild skin rashes with itching. **Contraindicated in pregnant women** (reduces the level of estrogen produced by the ovaries and the placenta), **or lactation women or medicating with contraceptives.**

Descriptions of plants letter W

- **Walnut tree / Nut**
- **Water Lily**
- **Weeping paperbark**
- **West Indian cherry**
- **White Chilean myrtle**
- **White mustard**

- White willow
- Wild mint
- Wood violet
- Withania aristata

- Walnut tree / Nut, (Nogal / Nueces, en español)

"Juglans regia", originating from Europe, the tree **sprout both female and male flowers**. It is used by consuming the fruit or the infusion of the leaves. **The leaf, applied to the skin can cause:** acne, eczema, ulcers and other skin infections. They can also lead to **excessive sweating of the hands and feet.** Applied assiduously **can cause cancer of the lips,** contain a substance called "jugione". **Do not consume excess nuts if you are following a diet** being rich in fat, being ideal to take weight. **Consumed in excess can cause:** skin rashes and swelling throughout the body, as well as nausea, stomach pain and diarrhea, in sensitive persons. **Contraindicated the essences and supplements of walnut by mouth, in pregnancy or lactation women, persons with gastritis or duodenal ulcers or consuming any medication. Contraindicated the nut, like an allergen, insecure in pregnancy or lactation women, asmatics.**

- Water Lily or Nymphaea, (Nenúfar, en español)

"Nymphaea", of the same species as the Lotus, but different plants, the Water Lily is at rest on the water, the Lotus seems to emerge from it. Used since antiquity from East to West, it grows in areas of stagnant water or streams without current and shallow depth. It is found in Southern Europe and North Africa. There are ointments, oils and Water Lily extracts, used for their healing properties, the root and flowers, in infusion. **Contraindicated in pregnant or lactation women, and under 12 years.**

- Weeping paperbark, (Cayeput, en español)

"Melaleuca leucadendra", a native tree from Southeast Asia and a tropical zone in Australia. **The best known use is in Inhalations, it is also used the infusion of the crust,** of analgesic properties, useful to reduce the ailments of aches and the headaches that usually accompany the colds. Its essential oil is greenish, camphorated and very penetrating. **Use very well diluted in a carrier oil** (Almonds or Sesame) is sufficient ...**Continue on next page**

... 10 drops per 100 ml of carrier oil. **Contraindicated in any way in under 6 years, and persons with respiratory allergies.**

- West Indian cherry, (Acerola, en español)

"Malpighia emarginata", fruit of a tree from South and Central America, and the Caribbean, is grown massively in Vietnam and Brazil. It has so many virtues beneficial to health, that we could say that it is a nutraceutical. **Pregnant women** should **not ingest it excessively**, or daily, **the baby** can become dependent and **develop symptoms of deficiency after birth.**

- Withania aristata, (Oroval, en español)

"Withania aristata", grows around the Mediterranean and especially in South Asia, endemic in the Canary Islands and North Africa, of the same species of Ashwagandha, the root, leaves and fruits are used. **Plant with some toxicity.** It is usually used the infusion of the root crust, the decoction of its fruits or the juice of the root. **It is recommended to consult with the doctor or specialist.**

- White Chilean myrtle, (Chequén, en español)

"Luma chequen", also know as Luma chequen, originating from Chile and Argentina, a very branched bush with a somewhat grayish crust, oval leaves, short and wide, all of which give off a soft fragrance, of solitary white flowers (endemic) that sprout of axillary form, and edible fruit, the stems, buds and leaves in infusion are used. **There are no known contraindications,** it is **recommended to consult** with the doctor or specialist.

- White mustard, (Mostaza blanca, en español)

"Sinapis alba" or "Brassica alba", originating from Mediterranean, the seeds and leaves are those that possess the medicinal qualities. There are preparations for different purposes, **even a sweet mustard made** for the little ones. You can consume the seed directly, sprinkling the meals and in infusions. **In topical use it can** generate inflammations in the skin. **Contraindicated in persons with inflammation and intestinal, urinary and stomach discomfort.**

- **Wild mint or Corn mint,** (Menta japonesa, en español)

"Mentha arvensis", originally from Asia, its appearance is similar to the European species, but stronger, it reaches a size of 40 cm in height, with leaves of green color and strong odor of Menthol. **It is recommended to consult with the doctor before using the essential oil** it can generate irritations in the eyes and on the skin. **To take advantage of its medicinal benefits,** place 2 or 3 drops of oil in 1 glass with warm water and take 2 times a day. You can also gargle with this preparation or warm it well and inhale the vapor. For external **use the oil esential droplets** can be placed in a cloth and passed in the affected area. **Contraindicated in pregnant or lactation women, and under 6 years and persons epileptics persons.**

- **White willow,** (Sauce blanco, en español)

"Salix alba", originating from Central and Southern Europe, North Africa and Western Asia. Willow crust has been used as a treatment for pain and fever in China since 500 B.C. The ancient Egyptians also used for inflammations. Due to other active components found in the crust, it is more effective than Aspirin (a synthetic derivative of the so-called acetylsalicylic acid that was developed and produced industrially by Germany in 1852), but stronger for the stomach. It is usually taken in infusion, in a cup with water add 1 or 2 tablespoons (of coffee) with crust, boil and for 10 minutes keep simmering, strain and drink 3 cups daily. **As side effects in high doses are cited:** ringing in the ears, ulcers, heartburn, pain, cramps, nausea, gastrointestinal bleeding and liver toxicity, rash, dizziness and kidney dysfunction. **There are capsules with white willow powder,** equally effective and healthier than Aspirin. Medical evidence indicates that the crust is less likely to cause gastrointestinal side effects as other pain relievers. **A lot of caution is recommended in pregnancy or lactation women, under 16 years especially with symptoms similar to the flu, chickenpox, or Reye's syndrome, persons with gout or asthma, allergic or sensitive to Aspirin. Avoid during the two weeks before or after any surgery.**

- Wood violet, (Violeta, en español)

"Viola odorata", originally from Asia and Europe, very beautiful flowers of violet or white (less habitual), of exquisite aroma and very delicate, very popular to ornament gardens and easy to cultivate. For the healing remedies the flowers and the rhizomes are used in infusion, there are specific preparations, essential oil and syrups. **In large doses causes:** vomiting, nervous problems and very serious circulatory. **Consult with the doctor or specialist for the consumption of pregnant women, under 12 years and persons with chronic health problems.**

Descriptions of plants letters Y - Z

- Yam
- Yarrow
- Yellow jessamine
- Yellow pepper
- Yellow trumpetbush
- Yerba mate
- Ylang Ylang

- Zucchini

- Yam, (Ñame silvestre, en español)

"Dioscorea alata" or "Dioscorea esculenta", originating from Africa and South Asia, it has been cultivated for thousands of years. **Considered for treatments of almost total female diseases.** The root and the bulb are used, the most common use is in capsules **(follow the indications of the specialist),** it exists in extracts or creams. **Contraindicated during pregnant women or suspects, in breastfeeding, under 6 years. Women with breast cancer, uterine endometrium, or uterine myomatosis.**

- Yarrow, (Aquilea o Milenrama, en español)

"Achillea millefolium", originating from Europe and the Middle East, it grows in meadows, hedges and meadow grass and is very aromatic, it used its leaves, flowers, essential oil, they exists in capsules. **In some cases topical use** may cause skin irritation. **Prolonged ingestion** may increase photosensitivity. **Contraindicated in pregnancy (abortive), or lactation.**

- Yellow jessamine, (Gelsemio, en español)

"Gelsemium sempervirens", also know as Carolina jasmine or Jessamine, original from Mexico and USA, vivacious climber of the family Gelsemiaceae is a **highly toxic plant that can be fatal if consumed in large quantities. Use only under medical prescription and pharmaceutical preparation.**

- Yellow pepper, (Pimiento amarillo, en español)

"Capsicum annuum", also know as California, originating from America. Its consumption is recommended with small quantities (3 or 5 gr.) of healthy oils such as olive oil, this combination favors the absorption of the carotenoids. A large yellow pepper provides approximately 1.7 gr. of dietary fiber, which represents 7% of the recommended daily value. **There are no known contraindications,** it is **recommended to consult** with the doctor or specialist

- Yellow trumpetbush, (Tronadora, en español)

"Tecoma stans", also know as Tecoma stans, originating from Mexico, of warm and mainly dry climates, grows around the edge of some roads in tropical forests. With leaves and yellow flowers in the shape of small bells that are grouped in beautiful and showy clusters, their fruits in the form of elongated capsules contain the seeds. It has 56 different chemical components in the leaves and flowers. Drink infusions made with leaves, branches, stems and even flowers and roots. **There are no known contraindications,** it is **recommended to consult** with the doctor or specialist.

- Yerba mate, (Mate, en español)

"Ilex paraguariensis", native to the Paraná basin and tributaries of the Paraguay River. It is consumed mainly in infusion, **at high doses it is narcotic and narcotic,** presenting headaches, dizziness, hypotension, respiratory failure. The essential oil is the main responsible for the toxicity of this plant. **Contraindicated in pregnancy or lactation women, under 12 years, patients with cardiac treatment, diabetes, glaucoma, gastritis, acidity, stomach ulcer, anxiety, insomnia, depressive, nervous disorders, hypertension.**

- Ylang Ylang or Cananga tree, (Ylang Ylang, en español)

"Cananga Odorata", tree native of Malaysia and means in Malay "flower of flowers", very aromatic flowers used to extract its essential oil in the healing remedies. **Use in topical use diluted in oil, shampoo, clay,** otherwise it may cause skin irritations. Also as inhalation through diffusers. There are creams, and prepared in specialized stores. **Excessive use can cause:** nausea or headaches, **keep it out** of reach of children. **Contraindicated in pregnant women.**

- Zucchini, (Calabacín, en español)

"Cucurbita pepo", also know as Summer squash, originating in Mesoamerica where it is known as "Zapallo de verano". Composed of 95% water, it does not have any caloric content, being highly beneficial for the organism. Studies have shown that 100 gr. of zucchini only contribute 15 gr. of calories, and contains a very good amount of minerals. **They should limit their consumption, persons suffering from kidney failure, taking diuretics, and children who have stomach problems, such as diarrhea.**

Bibliography

The Bibliography for the realization of this monograph is part of the one used in the book 8256 Natural Remedies, I want to make a special mention to the following sources:

- **Atlas of the Plants of Traditional Mexican Medicine**
- **Botanical dictionary of vulgar Cuban names, Carlos A. Martínez Bayón.**
- **Dioscórides, Plants and Medicinal Remedies (Of Medical Matter), Books I-III, Editorial Gredos, Translation and notes by Manuela García Valdés**
- **The Great Book of Medicinal Plants, M. Palow**
- **Everest Encyclopedia of Medicinal Plants**
- **Magazin Agrotechnical of Cuba, each plant is mentioned independently through EcuRed**

General Index

www.ingramcontent.com/pod-product-compliance
Lightning Source LLC
Chambersburg PA
CBHW061810250726
48657CB00001B/375